The Vegan Spiralizer
COOKBOOK

The Vegan Spiralizer Cookbook

CREATIVE, DELICIOUS, EASY RECIPES FOR EVERY MEAL

ROCKRIDGE
PRESS

TO MY FELLOW VEGANS:
THANK YOU FOR MAKING THE WORLD
A BETTER PLACE FOR ANIMALS.

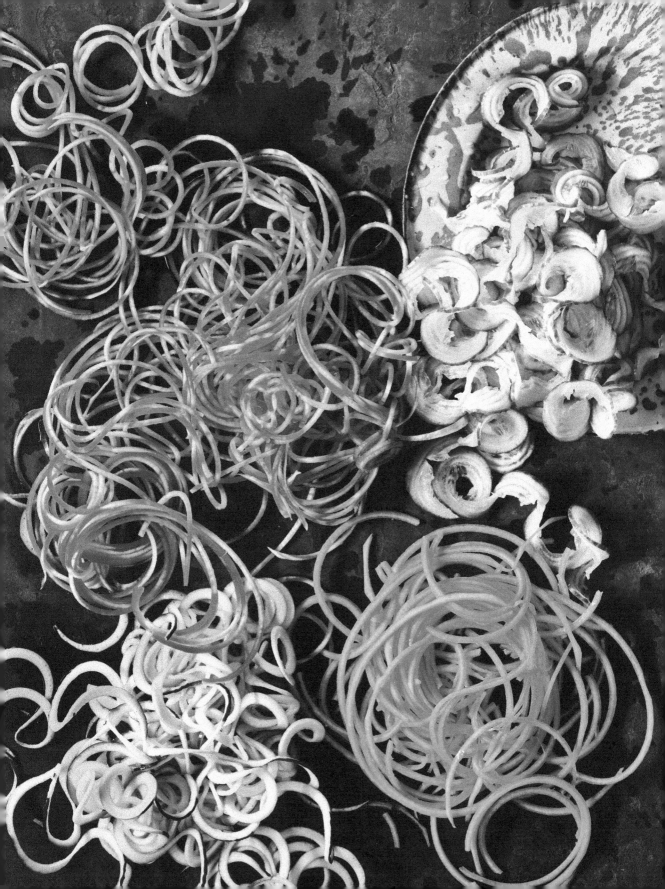

Contents

Introduction

What I love most about spiralizing is doing things in a slightly different way. You can change up the presentation of your favorite dishes without altering the flavor. And, as a bonus, you might even make them healthier (beets in chocolate cake, anyone?). I've been vegan since 2010, and although I eat a lot of fruits and vegetables, I know I could always eat more. Everyone, vegans and omnivores alike, needs vitamins and nutrients to keep our bodies healthy and strong, and including more fresh produce in our meals is a delicious way to get them.

My goal with this book is to present fresh ideas on how to prepare vegetables in fun, delicious ways, so we can all happily eat healthier. I've included traditional favorites and flavors inspired by my love of travel. I focused on fresh fruits and vegetables, healthy proteins (such as tofu and tempeh), and flavorful sauces to bring you 101 recipes that I hope you'll love as much as I do!

CHAPTER ONE

Ribbons, Spirals + Shoestrings

Welcome to the wonderful world of spiralizing, where the spiralizer is your secret weapon. Noodles, ribbons, spirals, rice—the shape doesn't really matter. What matters is that spiralizing helps you replace high-calorie ingredients, such as rice and pasta, with nutrient-dense veggies. It's true! We're not just making zoodles here; we're also making pizza crust from beets and rice from cauliflower. We're sneaking extra fruit—and flavor—into muffins and pancakes and making chocolate cake with beautiful red ribbons of beets. You're also about to start saving time and money! Spiralized vegetables tend to cook really quickly, much faster than their whole counterparts. And the fact that fruits and vegetables are just a fraction of the cost of meat is a happy bonus to go along with all the other benefits of a plant-based diet.

Whether you are new to spiralizing or have been zoodling for years, this book is designed to give you all the knowledge you need to create delicious, colorful, vegetable-forward meals. I'm sharing lots of tips and tricks to help get you started. We're going to cover which spiralizer model is best for your needs, which fruits and vegetables are best for spiralizing, and even how to use more vegan substitutes for the animal products you might be used to. The recipes I've created are easy to make and focus on fresh produce we all have access to. I'm so excited to share these recipes with you!

Which Spiralizer?

There are many different spiralizers on the market, but they all fall into one of two basic categories: the hand-crank model and the hourglass. I have one of each and use them both regularly. Both versions are affordable, with the most expensive hand-crank models coming in at under $50. Deciding which version to pull out of the cabinet usually depends on what I'm spiralizing and how much. Already a spiralizing pro? Read on for a refresher, or skip ahead to the recipes!

Hand-Crank Model

The hand-crank version attaches to your counter or tabletop with a suction cup and holds the fruit or vegetable in place while you turn the crank. The fruit or vegetable is pressed against the blade and quickly becomes a pile of delicious, nutritious spirals. These spiralizers come with multiple blades, usually between four and seven, so they offer flexibility. This is the one I use if I'm cooking a large amount of food or when I'm spiralizing a harder veggie such as sweet potato or butternut squash. Why? Because it's sturdier and requires less physical effort than the hourglass model.

One potential downside of the horizontal hand-crank model (where the fruit or vegetable is pressed sideways against the blade) is that it requires two hands to operate—one to apply sideways pressure toward the blade and one to turn the crank. There are vertical versions where the veggie is pressed down into the blade. This means gravity does some of the work for you, making these models a good choice for people who prefer not to or are unable to use both arms at once. If you own a KitchenAid stand mixer, you also have the option of using its spiralizer attachment.

Hourglass Model

The hourglass, or handheld spiralizer, is small and simple. It has two pieces, a handle and a part with blades that you place at either end of your vegetable and twist. There are fewer pieces to store (and wash!), and it's also generally lower-priced than its tabletop cousin. It does require more work on your part as you manually twist the pieces, and it works best on softer fruits and vegetables such as pears, zucchini, and cucumber. It's an excellent choice for veggie enthusiasts with limited storage space.

Spiralizing is easy and fun, but the blades are extremely sharp, so always be careful when handling them. Some people like to soak theirs, but my number one rule is to rinse and clean my blades immediately after use, before the food bits have time to dry out and get stuck to the metal. All you need is some hot water and dish soap. A small scrub brush can be your best friend—it'll fit into those tiny corners of your blades and protect your fingertips. Many spiralizers are also dishwasher safe, which makes it even easier! Just be sure to use the top rack and always keep the blades facing in the same direction to make unloading quicker and safer.

Which Veggies Can I Spiralize?

Some veggies are just better than others for spiralizing; it's like they were destined for it! Here are some of the most common vegetables you probably already cook with that I think you'll appreciate even more in their spiraled form: beets, bell peppers, broccoli stalks, butternut squash, cabbage, carrots, cucumbers, jicama (my favorite!), onions, parsnips, potatoes (all kinds, including sweet, which is my other favorite!), summer squash, and zucchini.

Fruits Are Good, Too!

Don't forget about the fruit! Apples, pears, and plantains are my favorite fruits to spiralize. With pears, especially, you don't want to choose ones that are too ripe. A firmer fruit yields a better ribbon, so choose ones that are just shy of fully ripe. With apples and other seeded fruits, you need to keep an eye on the seeds so they don't end up mixed in with your spirals. Fruits with pits can be a problem, but there are work-arounds. With mangos, for example, I like to cut large chunks away from the pit and spiralize them individually.

What Can't I Spiralize?

Fruits and vegetables that are really juicy (watermelon) or soft (peaches) just weren't meant for spiralizing. Anything small or with a hollow or soft core (like tomatoes) won't work well either because there just isn't enough to spiralize. This doesn't mean they can't be part of your new favorite zoodle dish, though! You can always dice, chop, or grate them and sprinkle them on top.

Which Veggies Are Best?

When you're cruising the produce department, there are a few things you should keep in mind. First is the width of the veggies, especially with long, thinner ones like carrots. Anything less than 1½ inches across won't work well with most blades.

Pro tip: If you want to spiralize carrots, you may have better luck choosing from among the loose carrots most grocers carry, so you can pick the largest ones. Bagged carrots contain many small ones you won't be able to spiralize.

You'll also want to keep an eye on length. Any produce less than 2 or 3 inches long won't yield enough ribbon to be worth it. I like to use my index finger as a measuring device when I'm in the grocery store!

Finally, consider the firmness of your vegetables. Firmer vegetables are easier to spiralize, so you need to find that sweet spot between not quite ripe and solid enough to create beautiful ribbons. You want your vegetable to feel firm but not actually hard.

Also, when working with vegetables like butternut squash, which vary in size from end to end, you're only working with the neck piece—not the bulbous end. So in recipes, size recommendations (like small, medium, or large squash) refer to the neck, not the whole squash.

Okay, Now How Do I Do It?

Whether you're using a tabletop/hand-crank or handheld/hourglass spiralizer, it's all about turning the veggie against the blade. Tabletop models have a pronged piece that holds the vegetable in place as you turn the crank, providing pressure against the blade. Handheld spiralizers work much like a pencil sharpener, where your manual twisting results in ribbons.

Produce	How to Prepare	How to Cook	Benefits	Try This!
APPLE	Skin on, remove the stem, and trim the end flat	Baked; fried; raw	High in fiber and water; aids weight loss by making you feel full fast	Apple-Walnut Muffins (page 33)
BEET	Skin on or peeled; both ends removed	Water-sauté; serve raw in salads	Lowers blood pressure and may help fight inflammation	Beet Brownies (page 148)
JICAMA	Waxy rind trimmed off; rounded edges cut flat	Raw in salads or on top of noodle dishes	High in fiber and antioxidants	Bánh Mì Bowl (page 44)
PARSNIP	Skin on or peeled; one end trimmed flat	Bake as fries	High in vitamins C and K	Spicy Southwestern Parsnip Fries (page 58)
PEAR	No need to peel; trim the end flat	Baked; raw on salads	Rich in antioxidants and flavonoids	Coconut-Pear Pancakes (page 15)
SUMMER SQUASH	No need to peel; trim both ends flat	In noodle dishes, fried or baked	High in vitamins A, B6, and C	Salt-and-Pepper Summer Squash (page 60)
SWEET POTATO	Skin on or peeled; one end trimmed flat	Water-sauté fried or baked	High in fiber, vitamin C, and potassium	Curried Sweet Potato Bowl (page 43)
ZUCCHINI	No need to peel; trim both ends flat	In noodle dishes	Improves digestion, lowers blood sugar	Three-Alarm Chili with Millet (page 96)

Taking time to prep your fruits and veggies properly for spiralizing will make the whole process go smoothly. Most of my recipes call for leaving the skin on, which means that giving the food a good scrub is necessary. In some instances, like with butternut squash, you'll need to peel the vegetable first. Trimming the edges is also important. You need a flat base to "attach" to the prongs that hold the food in place.

Finally, you need to choose the correct blade. Different spiralizer models use different naming conventions for their blades, so for the purpose of this book, I've identified the blades by the type of noodle they create, such as Angel Hair or Coarse Shred. And, although each recipe does call for a specific blade, feel free to take creative license. If your picky eaters are partial to thick curls, then make your meals using the Curly Fry blade. If you prefer your vegetables nice and thin, use the Angel Hair blade. The purpose of this book is to help you easily incorporate more healthy fruits and vegetables into your cooking; you know what works best for you and your family.

Making the Cut

Between the blades that came with your spiralizer and other kitchen tools you already have at your disposal (knives, food processors, mandolines, vegetable peelers, etc.), if you can imagine it, you can create it. Fettucine, spaghetti, and angel hair are all types of pasta you're likely familiar with, and you can make them with vegetables, too. Creating chips and curly fries from all sorts of veggies, not just potatoes, is possible (check out my Spicy Southwestern Parsnip Fries on page 58 for some inspiration!). You can even make rice! Veggies like cauliflower quickly turn to rice using a flat blade, while others may need a little help from the food processor. As I mentioned earlier, the exact blade names differ among manufacturers, so be sure to read the instruction booklet that came with your spiralizer to ensure you're getting the most out of it.

Many recipes also include instructions on trimming the length of the noodles you've just created. This is almost always presented as a range and is intended to make the noodles easier to work with.

Substitutions Galore!

Speaking of rice, spiralizing fruits and veggies is a great way to create new building blocks for all the dishes you make—not just the recipes in this book. Veggie rice can be served as a nutritious side dish, or it can be turned into pizza crust and flatbread. Zucchini becomes spaghetti, and sweet potatoes are suddenly pad Thai noodles. Whether you're trying to cut back on calories or want to sneak more veggies onto your loved ones' plates, spiralizing helps change the way you cook. I want to make it easy for you to eat more plant-based meals and create delicious, nutritious meals where your favorite veggies are the star, not just an afterthought.

On the Subject of Substitutions . . .

I've been vegan since 2010, and in that time, I've seen the market for vegan specialty items like cheese, ice cream, and plant "meats" explode! I enjoy these products and love how easy they are to find in most grocery stores these days. If you're familiar with my blog, you already know I use these products in my cooking, and some of the recipes in this book do call for vegan specialty products. Some of my favorite recipes with these kinds of ingredients include the Sausage and Zucchini Noodle Lasagna Casserole (page 121; which calls for vegan Italian sausage), and the Chick'n Fajitas (page 136; which are made with soy curls). Now, maybe you don't have any vegan Italian sausage on hand, or perhaps you don't really enjoy soy curls. That's fine! I've included tips for substituting these ingredients. So, for example, you could use baked tofu with Montreal chicken seasoning in the fajitas or just add extra veggies. Chapter 10 focuses on staples and sauces, all of which are vegan substitutes for traditional dairy items such as Alfredo Sauce (page 172; made with tofu!) and Coconut Whipped Cream (page 176; made with coconut milk!). They are used in recipes throughout the book. Of course, you can use store-bought vegan versions of these if you don't have time to make your own, but I hope you'll find the recipes helpful in your cooking adventures.

A quick note on egg substitutions in this book: For a long time, vegan egg substitutes were just mashed banana or applesauce in place of eggs in baked goods or chia seeds mixed with water. There are now quite a few "egg products" on the market. My favorite brands are Follow Your Heart and Just. Most recipes in this book were written using Follow Your Heart.

Many of my recipes also include tips for creating a meal that meets your requirements, whether that's being nut free or gluten free or even just replacing a vegetable you're unable to find (or don't particularly like).

Finally, you may notice some recipes use oil to sauté, whereas others stay light by using water. I'm not an oil-free vegan, but I like to use healthy hacks where I can, and using water to sauté veggies is one of them. Sometimes, though, I think using oil really adds something to a dish, whether flavor or texture, and so that's what the recipe calls for. You can always substitute water for sautéing; however, your results may differ.

What's Left Over?

After your favorite ingredients have made their way through your spiralizer, you'll notice you're left with the (mostly) inedible parts, such as the rinds and cores. Rather than sending these to the landfill or down your garbage disposal, consider composting. There are plenty of countertop composting setups that don't take up too much space, and the bonus is free fertilizer for your garden (which means more fruits and veggies to spiralize . . . it's a delicious cycle!). If composting isn't for you, keep a large resealable plastic bag in your freezer and add your vegetable scraps to it each time you spiralize. When it's full, make your own vegetable stock! Homemade stock is easy and delicious and much lower in sodium than most store-bought options, plus it will make your kitchen smell amazing. A good rule of thumb is to use a 1:1 ratio of veggies to water and simmer your stock for at least 45 minutes before straining out the vegetables.

Kitchen Gadgets

As a food blogger, I spend a lot of time playing around in the kitchen, but that doesn't mean I'm a collector of the latest and trendiest kitchen gadgets. In fact, it's quite the opposite. I tend to stick with simple, quality tools that serve more than one purpose. I think you'll see that reflected in this book as well. Other than the spiralizer itself, the tools these recipes call for are likely already in your kitchen! That said, here are a few things I find helpful in my kitchen to create these recipes.

1. **QUALITY KNIVES.** You're going to be prepping a lot of fruits and vegetables, and a dull knife can be dangerous (especially with large, thick veggies). I recommend stainless steel or ceramic-coated blades, as they can go years without needing sharpening.

2. **WOODEN CUTTING BOARDS.** They hold on to less bacteria than plastic boards and are easier on your knives than bamboo (which is a harder surface).

3. **SMALL BRISTLE BRUSH.** I mentioned this earlier, but it bears repeating: Spiralizer blades are sharp and can be time-consuming to clean by hand. A small brush that can get into the crevices will save you time and protect your fingers!

4. **POWERFUL BLENDER.** I would never recommend a $400 blender to anyone, and, honestly, if you have a blender that is getting the job done, stick with it. But when you're in the market for a new blender, I definitely recommend upgrading to a more powerful model. Prices have come down recently, and you can score one that can blend nearly anything for around $100.

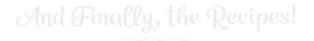

And Finally, the Recipes!

Many of the recipes I've shared in this book are nut and gluten free, and others include tips on how to make substitutions. Because fruits and vegetables are the stars of these recipes, the substitutions are often as simple as using a different type of nondairy milk or omitting nuts. My advice is never be afraid to make changes to a recipe. Be creative and make these recipes work for you! Try new vegan substitutions for animal products. Visit your local farmers' market and experiment with new fruits and veggies. Most importantly, you're about to start creating delicious, healthy, vegan meals that everyone will love, so give yourself a pat on the back, grab your spiralizer, and let's get started!

CHAPTER TWO

Breakfast

Cinnamon and Sweet Potato Waffles with Fresh Fruit, page 16

Apple-Cinnamon Pancakes

SERVES 4
Prep time: 7 minutes
Cook time: 8 minutes

1 cup all-purpose flour

2 tablespoons sugar

2 teaspoons
baking powder

½ teaspoon salt

½ teaspoon ground
cinnamon, plus more
for topping

1 cup nondairy milk

1 tablespoon apple cider
vinegar

1 teaspoon vanilla extract

1 apple

1 to 2 tablespoons vegan
butter, plus more for
topping

Pure maple syrup, for
topping

Pancakes have always been my favorite breakfast food, especially when they're dressed up a bit with delicious toppings . . . and what is more delicious than cinnamon and fresh apple? I recommend a sweet, crisp apple like Pink Lady or Honeycrisp.

1. In a medium bowl, stir together the flour, sugar, baking powder, salt, and cinnamon.

2. In another medium bowl, whisk together the milk, vinegar, and vanilla. Slowly add the dry ingredients to the wet ingredients, stirring well to ensure there are no lumps.

3. Spiralize the apple using the Coarse Shred blade and trim the spirals to 1- to 2-inch lengths. Gently fold about two-thirds of the apple into the batter.

4. Heat a large skillet or griddle over medium heat until hot.

5. Add the butter and let it melt completely. Spoon the batter into the skillet in desired portions, being sure to leave space between each pancake. Cook for 2 to 3 minutes, until bubbles begin to pop on the surface. Flip and cook the second side for 1 to 2 minutes more until done.

6. Top with the remaining apple and a sprinkle of cinnamon, plus butter and maple syrup, as desired.

Per serving: Calories: 226; Total fat: 4g; Total carbs: 43g; Fiber: 3g; Sugar: 12g; Protein: 4g; Sodium: 412mg

Coconut-Pear Pancakes

SERVES 4

Prep time: 7 minutes

Cook time: 8 minutes

1 cup nondairy milk

1 tablespoon apple cider vinegar

1 cup all-purpose flour

2 teaspoons baking powder

½ teaspoon salt

Dash ground cinnamon

1 teaspoon vanilla extract

1 pear

2 tablespoons shredded coconut, plus more for topping

1 to 2 tablespoons vegan butter, plus more for topping

Pure maple syrup, for topping

These sweet pancakes are perfect for holidays or when you want to give someone you love a special treat. The coconut and pear combination brings a delicious lightness to a food that can often seem heavy. When you're choosing your pear, pick one that's just a tiny bit shy of perfectly ripe: The extra firmness will make it easier to spiralize.

1. In a small bowl, stir together the milk and vinegar and let sit for 2 to 3 minutes. This is "vegan buttermilk."

2. In a large bowl, stir together the flour, baking powder, salt, and cinnamon. Slowly stir in the "buttermilk" and vanilla, stirring well to ensure there are no lumps.

3. Spiralize the pear using the Coarse Shred blade and trim the spirals into 1- to 2-inch lengths. Gently fold about two-thirds of the pear and the coconut into the batter.

4. Heat a large skillet or griddle over medium heat.

5. Add the butter and let it melt completely. Spoon the batter into the skillet, leaving space between each pancake. Cook for 2 to 3 minutes, until bubbles begin to pop on the surface. Flip and cook the second side for 1 to 2 minutes more, until done.

6. Top with the remaining pear and coconut, plus butter and maple syrup, as desired.

Per serving: Calories: 234; Total fat: 8g; Total carbs: 34g; Fiber: 3g; Sugar: 4g; Protein: 5g; Sodium: 451mg

Cinnamon and Sweet Potato Waffles with Fresh Fruit

SERVES 2

Prep time: 5 minutes
Cook time: 25 minutes

1 large sweet potato

2 to 3 tablespoons water

1½ teaspoons ground cinnamon

Pinch salt

1 very ripe banana

Nonstick cooking spray

Vegan butter, for topping

Fresh fruit, for topping

Pure maple syrup,
for topping

I realize that waffles made of sweet potatoes may sound . . . strange, but I promise they are delicious! The sweetness of the potatoes. The richness of the cinnamon. And then all that fruit? Perfection! Any fruit will work for a topping, but as you can already taste the banana, I recommend strawberries or blueberries.

1. Spiralize the sweet potato using the Angel Hair blade.

2. In a large skillet over medium-high heat, heat the water. Add the sweet potato spirals and sprinkle with the cinnamon and salt. Sauté for 5 to 6 minutes, or until just barely soft, letting the water cook off. Transfer the sweet potato spirals to a large bowl and let cool slightly.

3. In a small bowl, mash the banana with a fork. Mix the banana with the sweet potato spirals, using your hands to make sure there are no banana lumps left.

4. Preheat your waffle iron according to the manufacturer's instructions, and spritz it with cooking spray. Add the sweet potato mixture and close the lid. Cook until crispy. The exact time will depend on your waffle iron, but with mine, the waffle is done when the steam stops, 8 to 10 minutes. Repeat with the remaining batter.

5. Top with butter, fruit, and syrup.

Cooking tip: You'll want to use nonstick spray with this recipe: The sweet potato and banana combo is sticky!

Per serving: Calories: 115; Total fat: 1g; Total carbs: 28g; Fiber: 4g; Sugar: 10g; Protein: 2g; Sodium: 114mg

Apple-Pear Oatmeal with Granola

SERVES 2

Prep time: 6 minutes

Cook time: 5 minutes

1 apple

1 pear

1 cup nondairy milk
or a combination of milk
and water, plus more as
needed

½ cup rolled oats (not
instant)

¼ teaspoon salt

1 tablespoon light brown
sugar, plus more to taste

½ cup granola

Adding fresh fruit like apples and pears gives this oatmeal an extra boost, making this dish an excellent way to start your day. Spiralize the pear first, as the apple goes brown faster. If you want smaller fruit bits, cut them into shorter lengths. Use sweetened granola or sweetened milk, if you like, but using both will make it too sweet.

1. Spiralize the pear and apple using the Fine Shred blade and trim the spirals to 1- to 2-inch lengths.

2. In a medium saucepan over medium-high heat, heat the milk to a low boil, stirring frequently—don't let it scald.

3. Reduce the heat to low, stir in the oats, and cook for 1 minute.

4. Add the salt and three-fourths of the pear and apple spirals. Cover the pan and remove it from the heat. Let sit for 2 minutes.

5. Stir in the brown sugar and add another tablespoon of milk or water, if needed.

6. Spoon the oatmeal into bowls, and top with the granola and the remaining pear and apple.

Per serving: Calories: 290; Total fat: 6g; Total carbs: 55g; Fiber: 9g; Sugar: 26g; Protein: 6g; Sodium: 481mg

Carrot Cake Oatmeal

SERVES 2

Prep time: 6 minutes

Cook time: 6 minutes

1 large carrot

1 cup coconut milk, cashew milk, or a combination of milk and water, plus more as needed

½ cup rolled oats (not instant)

¼ cup raisins

¼ cup chopped walnuts, plus more for topping (optional)

2 tablespoons light brown sugar

½ teaspoon vanilla extract

¼ teaspoon salt, plus more as needed

Shredded coconut, for topping (optional)

Pure maple syrup, for topping (optional)

I've always considered putting vegetables in a cake to be cheating, but vegetables in oatmeal? Well, that sounds fair (and delicious) to me! This recipe proves oatmeal doesn't have to be plain or boring. And although we should probably skip the cream cheese frosting (because it is breakfast, after all), you should absolutely have some fun with toppings. Coconut, maple syrup, or even some chopped (or spiralized!) apples would all be great.

1. Spiralize the carrot using the Fine Shred blade and trim the spirals to about 1-inch lengths.

2. In a medium saucepan over medium-high heat, heat the milk to a low boil, stirring frequently—don't let it scald.

3. Stir in the oats and carrot spirals and cook for 1 minute.

4. Stir in the raisins, walnuts, brown sugar, vanilla, and salt. Cover the pan and remove it from the heat. Let sit for 3 to 4 minutes. If needed, stir in another tablespoon of milk to thin the consistency.

5. Spoon the oatmeal into bowls and top as desired.

Per serving: Calories: 196; Total fat: 2g; Total carbs: 41g; Fiber: 4g; Sugar: 22g; Protein: 4g; Sodium: 401mg

Tropical Plantain and Pineapple Oatmeal

SERVES 2

Prep time: 8 minutes

Cook time: 5 minutes

1 medium plantain

1 cup coconut milk, or a combination of milk and water

½ cup rolled oats (not instant)

1 tablespoon light brown sugar, plus more as needed

¼ teaspoon vanilla extract

¼ teaspoon salt

⅓ cup diced pineapple, canned or fresh

Shredded coconut, for topping (optional)

Golden raisins, for topping (optional)

Macadamia nuts, for topping (optional)

Plantains always make me think of Puerto Rico because that's where I first fell in love with them. I had only tried them fried and mashed; it wasn't until I started playing around with my spiralizer that I realized they had so much more potential. Their sweetness, along with the pineapple, is a nice addition to these oats. Love them as much as I do? Definitely check out the Tropical Plantain Bowl (page 39), too!

1. Spiralize the plantain using the Fine Shred blade and trim the spirals to about 1-inch lengths.

2. In a medium saucepan over medium-high heat, heat the milk to a low boil, stirring frequently—don't let it scald.

3. Stir in the oats and plantain spirals and cook for 1 minute. Remove from the heat and let sit for 2 to 3 minutes, or until thickened.

4. Stir in the brown sugar, vanilla, salt, and pineapple, and serve topped as desired.

Ingredient tip: Plantains are very much like bananas: You can tell they're ripe when they turn yellow with small black spots. Plantains that have turned almost entirely black will be too ripe (soft) to spiralize, so choose one that is still mostly yellow.

Per serving: Calories: 237; Total fat: 3g; Total carbs: 51g; Fiber: 5g; Sugar: 21g; Protein: 5g; Sodium: 377mg

Fruitful Quinoa

SERVES 2

Prep time: 5 minutes

Cook time: 22 minutes

1 cup cashew milk, plus more as needed

½ cup quinoa, rinsed well

2 tablespoons light brown sugar, plus more as needed

¼ teaspoon salt, plus more as needed

1 pear

1 apple

½ cup fresh blueberries

Pure maple syrup, for topping

If you had told me two years ago that I would be eating quinoa for breakfast, I would've called you crazy. Quinoa is just for savory dishes, right? Wrong. Quinoa is for *everything*! You can dress up its naturally mild flavor any way you like, especially with fresh fruit and maple syrup. If you're feeling adventurous, try cinnamon or cardamom sprinkled on top!

1. In a medium saucepan over medium-high heat, heat the milk to a low boil, stirring frequently—don't let it scald.

2. Stir in the quinoa and let the liquid return to a boil. Immediately reduce the heat to low and cover the pan. Simmer the quinoa for 15 minutes. There should be some milk left in the pan; if not, add another 1 to 2 tablespoons.

3. Remove the pan from the heat and stir in the brown sugar and salt. Cover the pan and let sit for 5 minutes.

4. Spiralize the pear and apple using the Fine Shred blade. Mix the pear and apple spirals together on a cutting board, and run a knife through them a few times in alternating directions until the pieces are 1 inch or smaller.

5. Stir the fruit into the quinoa along with more milk, as needed, to make it as creamy as you'd like. Allow the fruit and milk to warm before serving, and top with blueberries and maple syrup.

Per serving: Calories: 322; Total fat: 4g; Total carbs: 68g; Fiber: 9g; Sugar: 31g; Protein: 7g; Sodium: 378mg

Breakfast Burritos

SERVES 4 TO 6
Prep time: 15 minutes
Cook time: 35 minutes

For the tofu scramble

1 medium Yukon gold potato

1 bell pepper, any color

1 to 2 tablespoons water

½ sweet onion, diced

Nonstick cooking spray

1 (14-ounce) package firm tofu, drained and pressed for 15 to 20 minutes

2 to 3 tablespoons nondairy milk

½ cup vegan cheddar shreds

1 tablespoon nutritional yeast

1 teaspoon ground cumin

½ teaspoon *kala namak* salt

½ teaspoon red pepper flakes

1 tablespoon vegetable oil

⅛ teaspoon salt

⅛ teaspoon freshly ground black pepper

Who doesn't love a breakfast burrito? Is it weird that I hardly ever eat them for breakfast? I like to make a double batch, freeze the extras, and eat them at work for lunch! I roll them individually in aluminum foil and freeze them all in a large resealable plastic bag. When I take one to work, I let it thaw and reheat it in the toaster oven.

To make the tofu scramble

1. Preheat the oven to 350°F. Line a baking sheet with parchment paper.

2. Spiralize the potato and bell pepper using the Fine Shred blade.

3. In a large skillet over medium heat, heat the water. Add the onion and sauté for 1 to 2 minutes.

4. Add the bell pepper spirals and cook for 2 to 3 minutes. Drain any remaining water from the skillet, and push the veggies to the edges of the pan.

5. Spritz a little cooking spray into the center of the skillet, and crumble in the tofu.

6. Add the milk (use more or less depending on how soft you like your scramble), cheddar shreds, nutritional yeast, cumin, *kala namak* salt, and red pepper flakes. Stir to combine evenly.

For the burritos

4 to 6 large tortillas

1 (16-ounce) can vegetarian refried beans

1 cup vegan cheddar shreds

Salsa, for serving

7. Stir in the veggies to incorporate. Cook for 2 to 3 minutes, until the scramble is heated through. Remove the scramble from the pan and set aside.

8. Wipe the skillet clean, return it to medium heat, and heat the vegetable oil until it shimmers.

9. Add the potato spirals. Cook for 5 to 6 minutes, or until they're crispy, stirring as needed. Season to taste with salt and pepper.

To make the burritos

1. Layer the beans, potatoes, tofu scramble, cheddar shreds, and as much salsa as you'd like onto each tortilla.

2. Roll up the tortillas, and place them on the prepared baking sheet, seam-side down. Bake for 15 to 20 minutes, turning once.

Preparation tip: Worried about leftover burritos getting soggy? As soon as they're rolled, spritz them lightly with nonstick cooking spray before putting them in the oven. They'll crisp up (sort of like baked chimichangas) and won't be soggy when you reheat them.

Per serving: Calories: 527; Total fat: 22g; Total carbs: 62g; Fiber: 12g; Sugar: 5g; Protein: 23g; Sodium: 1219mg

Zucchini Fritters

SERVES 4

Prep time: 15 minutes

Cook time: 15 minutes

4 medium to large
zucchini

1 teaspoon salt, divided

1 vegan egg (my favorites
are Follow Your Heart and
Just)

½ cup chickpea flour

¼ cup nutritional yeast

¼ teaspoon garlic powder

⅛ teaspoon freshly
ground black pepper

1 to 2 tablespoons
vegetable oil

You know that point we all reach every summer, where every single person we know is gifting us zucchini and we've run out of ways to prepare it for lunch and dinner? Well, here's your chance to try it for breakfast! These fritters are flavorful, healthy, and easy to make.

1. Spiralize the zucchini using the Fine Shred blade and trim the spirals to 2- to 3-inch lengths. Put the zoodles in a colander and toss with 1 teaspoon of salt. Let sit for 10 to 15 minutes. As the salt pulls out some of the excess liquid from the zucchini, use a paper towel to squeeze out the rest. *You want the zoodles bone-dry—I cannot stress this enough.*

2. In a large bowl, stir together the zoodles, egg, flour, nutritional yeast, garlic powder, and pepper. Mix well.

3. In a large skillet over medium-high heat, heat 1 to 2 tablespoons of vegetable oil until it shimmers.

4. Add small scoops, about ¼ cup each, of the zucchini mixture to the skillet. (If the mix has become soupy because you had extra-juicy squash, squeeze out a little liquid before placing the batter in the pan.) Press the fritters flat with a spatula. If they're too thick, they won't cook all the way through. They should be about ¼-inch thick. Cook for 2 to 3 minutes, until golden brown. Flip and cook for 1 to 2 minutes more. Transfer to a paper towel to soak up any extra oil.

5. Add more oil to the skillet, and repeat as many times as necessary. Serve hot.

Per serving: Calories: 207; Total fat: 9g; Total carbs: 22g; Fiber: 8g; Sugar: 5g; Protein: 14g; Sodium: 350mg

Green Chile Hash Browns

SERVES 4

Prep time: 10 minutes
Cook time: 12 minutes

2 small to medium russet potatoes

1½ teaspoons cornstarch

½ cup diced roasted green chiles, canned or fresh

¾ teaspoon sea salt

½ teaspoon onion powder

½ teaspoon garlic powder

¼ teaspoon freshly ground black pepper

¼ cup vegetable oil

Breakfast, lunch, dinner, or snack, I'm always down to eat potatoes. I'm especially excited about these hash browns, because they're crispy, salty, and just a little bit spicy from the green chiles. Plus, they're versatile! Serve them with fresh fruit and toast or with the Veggie Frittata (page 27).

1. Spiralize the potatoes using the Angel Hair blade. Wrap the potato spirals in paper towels and squeeze gently to remove excess liquid. Transfer to a large bowl and toss with the cornstarch. Let sit for 2 to 3 minutes.

2. Stir in the green chiles, salt, onion powder, garlic powder, and pepper.

3. In a large skillet over medium heat, heat the vegetable oil until it shimmers.

4. Add the potato mixture in four separate scoops. Flatten each into a round patty of ¼-inch thickness, and cook for 5 to 6 minutes, or until the bottom side is golden brown.

5. Carefully flip, so as not to break them apart, and cook for 5 to 6 minutes more.

6. Transfer to paper towels to drain for a minute or so before serving.

Ingredient tip: Russets are great for hash browns because of their high starch content.

Per serving: Calories: 241; Total fat: 14g; Total carbs: 27g; Fiber: 3g; Sugar: 3g; Protein: 4g; Sodium: 598mg

Cranberry-Maple Sweet Potato Hash

SERVES 4

Prep time: 10 minutes

Cook time: 15 minutes

1 large sweet potato

2 tablespoons water

¼ cup unsweetened dried cranberries

2 tablespoons pure maple syrup

½ teaspoon salt, plus more as needed

¼ teaspoon freshly ground black pepper

2 tablespoons vegan butter

I grew up in New Hampshire, and when I was little, we lived down the road from a farm. Springtime was sugaring season, when the farmers would tap the maple trees, collect the sap, and make fresh maple syrup. Whenever I could sneak out of the house, I'd loiter around the "sugaring shack," hoping to be invited in for a taste. I add real maple syrup to recipes whenever I can. It's the perfect foil for the tart cranberries in this hash, and you'll love the way it tastes after caramelizing in the hot pan.

1. Spiralize the sweet potato using the Angel Hair blade and trim the spirals to 1- to 2-inch lengths.

2. In a large nonstick skillet over medium heat, heat the water. Add the sweet potato spirals and sauté for 4 to 5 minutes. Transfer to a large bowl, and stir in the cranberries, maple syrup, salt, and pepper.

3. Return the same skillet to medium-high heat and melt the butter.

4. Add the sweet potato mixture, spreading it evenly throughout the pan, using a spatula to press it down. Cook for 4 to 5 minutes, without stirring, or until the sweet potatoes start to brown. Flip the sweet potatoes, and cook for 4 minutes more, or until evenly browned and crispy. Serve hot.

Per serving: Calories: 107; Total fat: 6g; Total carbs: 14g; Fiber: 1g; Sugar: 8g; Protein: 1g; Sodium: 319mg

Veggie Frittata

SERVES 6

Prep time: 25 minutes

Cook time: 45 minutes

Nonstick cooking spray

1 medium to large butternut squash

2 small Yukon gold potatoes

3 to 4 tablespoons water

1 small sweet onion, diced

2 Roma tomatoes, roughly diced

2 cups packed fresh baby spinach leaves

1 (14-ounce) block firm tofu, drained (not pressed)

¼ cup unsweetened nondairy milk

¼ cup nutritional yeast

2 tablespoons cornstarch

½ teaspoon *kala namak* salt

½ teaspoon garlic powder

¼ teaspoon salt, plus more for seasoning

¼ teaspoon freshly ground black pepper, plus more for seasoning

1 cup vegan cheddar shreds

Frittatas are one of those dishes I never tried before going vegan, but now that I've started making them with tofu, I can't get enough! I love all the combinations of vegetables you can include, so don't be afraid to make substitutions (Kale for spinach! Sweet potato for Yukon gold!). One ingredient you should definitely stick with, though, is the *kala namak* salt, which is what makes this vegan frittata taste like egg. You can find it at most specialty spice stores or online.

1. Preheat the oven to 375°F. Coat a 9-inch springform pan with cooking spray.

2. Cut off the bulbous end of the butternut squash and reserve for another use. Trim the ends of the remaining neck piece, and slice or peel off the rind. Spiralize the squash and the potatoes using the Coarse Shred blade.

3. In a large nonstick skillet over medium heat, heat the water. Add the onion and sauté for 2 minutes.

4. Add the squash and potato spirals, and continue to cook for 5 to 6 minutes more, stirring frequently as the veggies start to cook down; add more water if the pan gets dry.

5. Stir in the tomatoes and spinach, and cook for 2 to 3 minutes. Remove the pan from the heat and set aside.

CONTINUED

6. In a blender or food processor, combine the tofu, milk, nutritional yeast, cornstarch, *kala namak* salt, garlic powder, salt, and pepper. Pulse until smooth, stopping to scrape down the sides with a spoon or rubber spatula, as needed. Pour the tofu mixture over the veggies and add the cheddar shreds. Stir to combine.

7. Pour the mixture into the prepared pan and bake for 35 to 40 minutes, or until firm to the touch. Let cool for 5 minutes before serving.

Preparation tip: Springform pans are great because they keep your frittata neat and perfect; if you don't have one, use a 9-inch baking dish.

Per serving: Calories: 256; Total fat: 8g; Total carbs: 37g; Fiber: 8g; Sugar: 5g; Protein: 14g; Sodium: 367mg

Banana-Apple Bread

MAKES 1 LOAF
Prep time: 10 minutes
Cook time: 1 hour

Nonstick cooking spray

2 cups all-purpose flour

½ teaspoon ground nutmeg

½ teaspoon ground cinnamon

½ teaspoon baking soda

½ teaspoon salt

½ cup vegan butter, at room temperature

¾ cup sugar

1 teaspoon vanilla extract

2 very ripe bananas, mashed with a fork

¼ cup nondairy milk

1 teaspoon apple cider vinegar

1 large apple

I don't bake very often. When it comes to fruity breads and muffins, though, I'm absolutely willing to make an exception—especially for this super-moist banana bread. The combination of nutmeg and cinnamon is delicious, and the spirals of apple give it extra flair!

1. Preheat the oven to 350°F. Coat the inside of a 9½-by-5-inch loaf pan with cooking spray. Set aside.

2. In a medium bowl, whisk together the flour, nutmeg, cinnamon, baking soda, and salt. Set aside.

3. In a large bowl, using a handheld electric mixer, cream together the butter and sugar.

4. Add the vanilla extract, mashed banana, milk, and vinegar, and mix on low speed just until completely blended.

5. Slowly add the dry ingredients to the wet ingredients, as you continue to mix on low speed; do not overmix.

6. Spiralize the apple using the Coarse Shred blade and gently fold the spirals into the batter. Pour the batter into the prepared pan.

7. Bake for 50 to 60 minutes, or until a toothpick inserted into the center of the loaf comes out clean.

8. Let cool for 10 minutes. Remove the loaf from the pan, and let cool on a wire rack before serving.

CONTINUED

Ingredient tip: Stick with crisp apple varieties like Pink Lady, Cripps, and Honeycrisp.

Per serving (⅛ loaf): Calories: 346; Total fat: 12g; Total carbs: 57g; Fiber: 3g; Sugar: 26g; Protein: 4g; Sodium: 372mg

Cinnamon-Zucchini Muffins

MAKES 12 MUFFINS
Prep time: 15 minutes
Cook time: 25 minutes

Nonstick cooking spray

1 small zucchini

½ cup vegetable oil

½ cup pure maple syrup

¾ cup nondairy milk, such as cashew

2 teaspoons apple cider vinegar

1 teaspoon vanilla extract

2 cups all-purpose flour

1½ cups oat flour

½ cup packed light brown sugar

2 teaspoons ground cinnamon

2 teaspoons baking powder

¼ teaspoon salt

There are some people who say muffins are just little cakes, and though *technically* they may be correct, I refuse to give in to their cynicism. Muffins are a totally acceptable, delicious breakfast in my book (see what I did there?), especially when they contain veggies.

1. Preheat the oven to 350°F. Coat a muffin pan with cooking spray, or fill it with paper liners. Set aside.

2. Spiralize the zucchini using the Angel Hair blade and trim the spirals to 1-inch lengths (you should have about one heaping cup of zoodles). Using a clean kitchen towel, gently squeeze out the excess liquid.

3. In a small bowl, whisk together the vegetable oil, maple syrup, milk, vinegar, and vanilla.

4. In a large bowl, stir together the all-purpose and oat flours, brown sugar, cinnamon, baking powder, and salt.

5. Stir the wet ingredients into the dry ingredients, using a whisk or rubber spatula. Don't overmix—it is a very thick batter. Spoon the batter into the prepared muffin cups, dividing it evenly.

6. Bake for 20 to 25 minutes, or until a toothpick inserted into the center of a muffin comes out clean.

CONTINUED

7. Let cool on a wire rack for 10 minutes. Remove muffins from the pan, and let cool before serving.

Per serving (1 muffin): Calories: 282; Total fat: 10g; Total carbs: 44g; Fiber: 2g; Sugar: 16g; Protein: 4g; Sodium: 64mg

Apple-Walnut Muffins

MAKES 12 MUFFINS
Prep time: 15 minutes
Cook time: 25 minutes

Nonstick cooking spray

½ cup vegetable oil

½ cup pure maple syrup

¾ cup unsweetened nondairy milk, such as cashew

2 teaspoons apple cider vinegar

1 teaspoon vanilla extract

3½ cups all-purpose flour

½ cup packed light brown sugar

1 teaspoon ground cinnamon

1 teaspoon ground nutmeg

1 teaspoon baking powder

¼ teaspoon salt

1 apple

½ cup chopped walnuts

2 to 3 tablespoons turbinado sugar

This combination of apple, cinnamon, and walnut is delicious. This is a very thick batter, but once done baking, these muffins are nice and fluffy! I went light on the turbinado sugar topping because these are intended for breakfast . . . but if you want to make them sweeter and fancier-looking, double that sugar!

1. Preheat the oven to 350°F. Coat a muffin pan with cooking spray, or fill it with paper liners. Set aside.

2. In a small bowl, whisk together the vegetable oil, maple syrup, milk, vinegar, and vanilla.

3. In a large bowl, stir together the flour, brown sugar, cinnamon, nutmeg, baking powder, and salt. Stir the wet ingredients into the dry ingredients, using a whisk or rubber spatula. Don't overmix.

4. Spiralize the apple using the Angel Hair blade and trim the spirals to 1-inch lengths. Using a clean kitchen towel, gently squeeze out the excess liquid. Fold the apple spirals and walnuts into the batter, then divide it equally among the prepared muffin cups. Sprinkle the muffin tops with the turbinado sugar.

5. Bake for 20 to 25 minutes, or until a toothpick inserted into the center of a muffin comes out clean.

6. Place the muffin tray on a wire rack and let cool for 10 minutes. Remove the muffins from the pan, and let them cool before serving.

Per serving (1 muffin): Calories: 344; Total fat: 13g; Total carbs: 54g; Fiber: 2g; Sugar: 20g; Protein: 5g; Sodium: 64mg

Bowls

Bánh Mì Bowl, page 44

Barbecue Tofu Bowl

SERVES 4

Prep time: 15 minutes, plus 1½ to 2 hours to press and marinate the tofu
Cook time: 35 minutes

1 (14-ounce) block firm tofu, drained and pressed for at least 1 hour, halved horizontally, then each piece halved widthwise (you'll have 4 small rectangles)

½ cup barbecue sauce

Nonstick cooking spray

2 small to medium sweet potatoes

¼ cup water

¼ teaspoon salt, plus more as needed

⅛ teaspoon freshly ground black pepper

½ batch Creamy Coleslaw (page 62)

This recipe feels like summer in a bowl. The rich, tangy barbecue sauce coating the baked tofu and the creamy coleslaw with just the right amount of zing—these are two of my favorite dishes to bring to summer parties and potlucks, and I've finally found a way to combine them! The sweet potato noodles (spoodles?) make the perfect base. They're hearty and filling, and I love the light sweetness combined with the barbecue sauce.

1. Put the tofu pieces in a small bowl, add the barbecue sauce, turn to coat, and let marinate for 30 to 60 minutes.

2. Preheat the oven to 400°F. Line a baking sheet with foil, and coat the foil with cooking spray.

3. Transfer the marinated tofu slices to the prepared baking sheet (reserve the sauce), and bake for 35 minutes. Halfway through the baking time, spritz the top of the tofu with more cooking spray, flip, and brush or spoon on another 1 to 2 tablespoons of the barbecue sauce.

4. Cut the baked tofu into bite-size cubes (I make eight per rectangle).

5. While the tofu bakes, spiralize the sweet potatoes using the Coarse Shred blade, and trim the spirals to 1- to 2-inch lengths.

6. In a large skillet over high heat, bring the water to a boil. Add the sweet potato spirals and sauté for 3 to 4 minutes, or until just barely tender. Drain any remaining water (if necessary), season with salt and pepper, and stir in the remaining barbecue sauce. Cover the skillet, remove it from the heat, and let the noodles sit in the sauce for 1 to 2 minutes.

7. To assemble the bowls, layer the sweet potato noodles, tofu cubes, and coleslaw.

Preparation tip: Pressing the tofu well is important! Removing as much water as possible will ensure "meatier," less mushy tofu cubes. It will also allow the tofu to soak up more of the sauce. Feeding an extra-hungry crowd? Double the tofu (and barbecue sauce) to make these bowls more filling.

Per serving: Calories: 271; Total fat: 10g; Total carbs: 39g; Fiber: 6g; Sugar: 20g; Protein: 11g; Sodium: 950mg

Quinoa Veggie Bowl with Garlicky Lemon Cream Sauce

SERVES 4

Prep time: 10 minutes

Cook time: 6 minutes

2 summer squash

1 zucchini

1 bell pepper, any color

2 tablespoons water

½ teaspoon salt

¼ teaspoon freshly ground black pepper

½ batch Garlicky Lemon Cream Sauce (page 174)

3 cups cooked quinoa, seasoned with salt and pepper

This bowl has become one of my go-tos for Sunday meal prep because it reheats so well for workday lunches. And though it's filling (and full of protein and fiber—thanks, quinoa!), it's also light. I appreciate not feeling weighed down and sleepy when I still have a full afternoon of work ahead of me. And because the sauce is really the star of the show, you can easily substitute other seasonal vegetables. Butternut squash and sweet potatoes are excellent choices.

1. Spiralize the summer squash, zucchini, and bell pepper using the Fine Shred blade.

2. In a large skillet over medium heat, heat the water. Add the squash, zucchini, and bell pepper spirals, season with salt and pepper, and sauté for 2 to 3 minutes.

3. Add the Garlicky Lemon Cream Sauce and reduce the heat to low. Simmer for 1 to 2 minutes, or until heated through.

4. Scoop the quinoa into four bowls, and top with the creamy veggies.

Substitution tip: I sometimes make this dish using millet and brown rice instead of quinoa, and it's still delicious!

Per serving: Calories: 330; Total fat: 9g; Total carbs: 52g; Fiber: 8g; Sugar: 4g; Protein: 12g; Sodium: 555mg

Tropical Plantain Bowl

SERVES 4

Prep time: 10 minutes
Cook time: 12 minutes

1½ teaspoons coconut oil, divided

1 small sweet onion, thinly sliced

3 garlic cloves, minced

1 red bell pepper, thinly sliced

4 cups torn baby kale leaves

¼ cup coconut milk, lite or full fat, plus more as needed

1 cup cooked or canned (rinsed and drained) black beans

1 tablespoon jerk seasoning

2 medium plantains

¼ teaspoon salt

⅛ teaspoon freshly ground black pepper

1 avocado, halved, pitted, and sliced

2 scallions, thinly sliced (green parts only)

1 lime, quartered

I discovered jerk seasoning right around the same time I discovered my love of travel. I still haven't been to Jamaica, where jerk seasoning is from, but it is used in many Caribbean countries, so to me, it tastes like vacation. It's primarily used on meats but is also amazing on vegetables, chickpeas, and, of course, mock meats. There's absolutely nothing keeping us vegans from getting our jerk on!

1. In a large skillet over medium-high heat, melt 1 teaspoon of coconut oil until it shimmers.

2. Add the onion and sauté for 1 to 2 minutes, stirring frequently.

3. Add the garlic and red bell pepper and cook, stirring frequently, for 2 to 3 minutes more, or until fragrant.

4. Stir in the kale, coconut milk, black beans, and jerk seasoning. Cover the skillet and remove it from the heat. When you're ready to build the bowls, add 1 to 2 tablespoons more milk if you want more sauce.

5. Spiralize the plantains using the Angel Hair blade.

6. In another large skillet over medium-high heat, melt the remaining ½ teaspoon of coconut oil until it shimmers.

CONTINUED

7. Add the plantain spirals, salt, and pepper. Cook, without stirring, for 1 to 2 minutes. Flip with a spatula (they're too delicate for stirring), and cook for 2 to 3 minutes more, flipping as needed, until they're crispy and slightly browned.

8. To build the bowls, layer the crispy plantain noodles, then the veggie mix. Top with avocado slices and scallions, and squeeze the lime wedges over the dish.

Ingredient tip: Jerk seasoning has quite a few ingredients, but the most flavor-forward are allspice and scotch bonnet—a spicy pepper. It's sweet and spicy and savory, all at once.

Per serving: Calories: 343; Total fat: 13g; Total carbs: 56g; Fiber: 11g; Sugar: 17g; Protein: 9g; Sodium: 164mg

Garlicky Chili Cauliflower Rice Bowl

SERVES 4

Prep time: 10 minutes
Cook time: 15 minutes

1 large head cauliflower

1 tablespoon olive oil

¼ teaspoon salt

⅛ teaspoon freshly ground black pepper

1 small sweet potato

2 tablespoons water

½ batch Garlicky Lemon Cream Sauce (page 174)

2 to 3 teaspoons Sriracha

1 (15.5-ounce) can chickpeas, rinsed and drained

Sliced scallions (green parts only), for topping (optional)

Chopped fresh herbs, for topping (optional)

If you're introducing someone to cauliflower rice, this is the dish to do it with. With the olive oil and a pinch of salt and pepper added, it tastes so rich, I sometimes eat it alone! It's a shame to do that, though, because the garlicky chili sauce is so delicious.

1. Using a box grater or a food processor, grate the cauliflower into rice-like pieces.

2. In a large nonstick skillet over medium heat, heat the olive oil until it shimmers.

3. Add the cauliflower rice, salt, and pepper. Cook for 5 to 6 minutes, stirring frequently. Remove from the skillet and set aside.

4. Spiralize the sweet potato using the Coarse Shred blade.

5. In the same skillet over medium heat, heat the water. Add the sweet potato spirals and sauté for 5 to 7 minutes, or just until soft.

6. While the sweet potato cooks, in a small bowl, stir together the Garlicky Lemon Cream Sauce and Sriracha. Set aside.

CONTINUED

7. When the sweet potatoes are done, reduce the heat to low and stir in the chickpeas and sauce.

8. Divide the cauliflower rice into four bowls. Top with the sweet potato spirals and desired toppings.

Per serving: Calories: 279; Total fat: 10g; Total carbs: 43g; Fiber: 11g; Sugar: 6g; Protein: 10g; Sodium: 760mg

Curried Sweet Potato Bowl

SERVES 4
Prep time: 10 minutes
Cook time: 15 minutes

2 medium sweet potatoes

1 tablespoon olive oil

2 garlic cloves, minced

½ teaspoon ground ginger

2 tablespoons Thai red curry paste

1 (14-ounce) can lite coconut milk

½ cup water

1 teaspoon salt

¼ teaspoon freshly ground black pepper

3 cups cooked brown rice, seasoned with salt and pepper

4 cups fresh baby spinach leaves, steamed

1 lime, quartered

Don't let the simplicity of this curry fool you! It's so rich and fragrant, it's like you spent all day preparing it. It makes excellent leftovers, too, as the flavors meld and become even better. Heat this up in the breakroom at work and your coworkers will be jealous. Not a fan of brown rice? Swap in your favorite grain or use cauliflower rice!

1. Spiralize the sweet potatoes using the Curly Fry blade, and trim the spirals to 3- to 4-inch lengths. Set aside.

2. In a large skillet over medium heat, heat the olive oil until it shimmers.

3. Add the garlic and sauté for 1 minute. Add the ginger and cook for 1 minute more. It should smell amazing!

4. Stir in the sweet potato spirals, curry paste, coconut milk, water, salt, and pepper. Cover the skillet and reduce the heat to maintain a simmer. Cook for 8 to 10 minutes, or until the sweet potatoes are cooked through.

5. Build your bowls with a layer of rice, followed by spinach, then top with the sweet potato mixture. Squeeze a lime wedge over each bowl.

Ingredient tip: Some curry pastes contain fish sauce, so be sure to check the ingredients!

Per serving: Calories: 304; Total fat: 12g; Total carbs: 48g; Fiber: 4g; Sugar: 4g; Protein: 6g; Sodium: 1044mg

Bánh Mì Bowl

SERVES 4

Prep time: 15 minutes, plus 1 hour to marinate the veggies and tofu

Cook time: 15 minutes

For the pickled veggies

2 medium carrots

1 medium jicama (about the size of an apple), rind removed

½ cucumber

¾ cup rice wine vinegar

1 teaspoon sesame oil

½ teaspoon salt

¼ cup plus 1 tablespoon sugar

For the tofu

¼ cup soy sauce

¼ cup rice wine vinegar

¼ teaspoon ground ginger

1 (14-ounce) block firm tofu, drained and pressed, halved horizontally, then each piece halved widthwise (you'll have 4 small rectangles)

1 tablespoon chili oil

I once spent an entire week in Vietnam without ever finding a vegan *bánh mì* sandwich! If you're a fan of the spicy, vinegary sandwich, too, you can imagine my disappointment. Luckily, even the vegan version is pretty easy to make at home. These days when I need a *bánh mì* fix, I go for the bowl version. Using quinoa instead of bread is a healthy substitution, and if you want to go a step further, replace the quinoa with sweet potato or carrot noodles.

To make the pickled veggies

1. Spiralize the carrots, jicama, and cucumber with the Coarse Shred blade and trim the spirals to 3- to 4-inch lengths.

2. In a large bowl, whisk together the vinegar, sesame oil, salt, and sugar. Add the veggie spirals and toss to combine. Cover the bowl and refrigerate for at least 1 hour (longer is better). Stir once or twice to make sure all the veggies are coated with the marinade.

To make the tofu

1. In a medium shallow bowl, whisk together the soy sauce, vinegar, and ginger. Add the tofu rectangles, cover the bowl, and let marinate for 1 hour.

2. In a large skillet over medium-high heat, heat the chili oil until it shimmers.

For the sauce

⅔ cup vegan mayonnaise

2 tablespoons leftover marinade

1 tablespoon Sriracha, plus more as needed

2 teaspoons hoisin sauce

For serving

3 cups cooked quinoa, seasoned with salt and pepper

1 jalapeño pepper, thinly sliced

Fresh cilantro, for topping

3. Add the tofu (reserve the marinade) and fry for 4 to 5 minutes per side, or until browned and crispy. Remove the tofu from the pan and let cool for a minute or two. Cut each rectangle into 6 to 8 cubes. Set aside.

To make the sauce

In a small bowl, stir together the mayonnaise, reserved marinade, Sriracha, and hoisin sauce.

To serve

To build the bowls, layer the quinoa, tofu cubes, and pickled veggies. Drizzle with the creamy sauce. Top with jalapeño and cilantro.

Ingredient tip: I use jicama in this recipe because I love its mild flavor (and it's easier to find where I live), but you can substitute the more traditional daikon if you prefer.

Per serving: Calories: 633; Total fat: 22g; Total carbs: 82g; Fiber: 15g; Sugar: 22g; Protein: 20g; Sodium: 1496mg

Spicy Thai Peanut Veggie Noodles

SERVES 4

Prep time: 10 minutes
Cook time: 10 minutes

For the sauce

½ cup creamy peanut butter

⅓ cup warm water

¼ cup lite soy sauce

2 tablespoons rice wine vinegar

2 to 4 teaspoons Thai chili paste (depending on your taste buds, start with 2 teaspoons and work your way up)

1 teaspoon brown sugar

½ teaspoon garlic powder

This creamy, spicy peanut sauce is so rich and comes together in a snap. I love how thickly it coats all the fresh veggies in this recipe. I wish I could add it to all my dishes! That said, if you're really short on time, never feel bad about using store-bought sauce. You can also pick up a package of baked tofu while you're at it, if you'd like to bulk up this bowl for some extra-hungry eaters. Farro is an amazing grain that is low in calories and high in fiber and provides 28 grams of protein per serving.

To make the sauce

In a medium bowl, whisk together the peanut butter, water, soy sauce, vinegar, chili paste, brown sugar, and garlic powder until smooth. Set aside.

To make the bowl

1. Spiralize the carrots, cucumber, and red bell pepper using the Coarse Shred blade.

2. In a large skillet over medium heat, heat the water. Add the carrot and red bell pepper spirals and sauté for 4 to 5 minutes, or just until soft.

3. Reduce the heat to medium-low and stir in the cucumber spirals and the sauce. Cook for 1 to 2 minutes, or until the cucumber is warmed through.

For the bowl

2 large carrots

1 cucumber

1 red bell pepper

2 tablespoons water

3 cups cooked farro

Juice of 1 lime

Zest of 1 lime

Bean sprouts, for topping (optional)

Fresh cilantro, for topping (optional)

Chopped peanuts, for topping (optional)

4. Add the lime juice.

5. To assemble your bowls, layer the veggies on top of the farro and sprinkle with lime zest. Add any optional toppings, as desired.

Substitution tip: If you don't have farro on hand, use brown rice or cauliflower rice. There are a few gluten-free versions of soy sauce available in stores as well, if gluten intake is a concern.

Per serving: Calories: 451; Total fat: 19g; Total carbs: 55g; Fiber: 10g; Sugar: 11g; Protein: 17g; Sodium: 912mg

Crispy Tofu Squash Bowl

SERVES 4

Prep time: 15 minutes

Cook time: 25 minutes

2 to 3 tablespoons vegetable oil

1 (14-ounce) package firm tofu, drained, pressed well, and cut into cubes

½ cup hoisin sauce, divided

1 teaspoon Sriracha, plus more for topping

1 medium butternut squash

2 to 3 tablespoons water

2 cups sliced baby bella mushrooms

2 garlic cloves, minced

½ teaspoon ground ginger

¼ teaspoon salt

Sliced scallions (green parts only), for topping (optional)

Sesame seeds, for topping (optional)

Getting your tofu crispy is the key to this dish. My mom turns up her nose at tofu that doesn't pass her crispiness test. I mean, she'll still eat it, but she makes a face. So I guess this Crispy Tofu Squash Bowl is for you, Mom!

1. In a large nonstick skillet over medium-high heat, heat 2 tablespoons of vegetable oil until it shimmers.

2. Add the tofu and cook until crispy and lightly browned, 2 to 3 minutes per side, adding the remaining 1 tablespoon of vegetable oil as needed.

3. Pour in ¼ cup of hoisin and the Sriracha, and stir the tofu to coat. Reduce the heat to low and simmer for 2 to 3 minutes. Remove from the heat.

4. Cut off the bulbous end of the butternut squash and reserve for another use. Trim the ends of the remaining neck piece and slice or peel off the rind. Spiralize the neck using the Coarse Shred blade.

5. In a medium skillet over medium-high heat, heat the water. Add the butternut squash spirals and sauté for 3 to 4 minutes.

6. Add the remaining ¼ cup of hoisin, mushrooms, garlic, ginger, and salt. Reduce the heat to medium-low and simmer for 3 to 4 minutes more, or until the squash and mushrooms are soft.

7. Spoon the noodles into four bowls, and top with the tofu and any desired toppings.

Per serving: Calories: 307; Total fat: 16g; Total carbs: 34g; Fiber: 5g; Sugar: 13g; Protein: 12g; Sodium: 593mg

Maple-Sriracha Tempeh Bowl

SERVES 4

Prep time: 15 minutes
Cook time: 15 minutes

¼ cup pure maple syrup

2 tablespoons Sriracha

1 (8-ounce) package tempeh, cut into bite-size pieces

1 tablespoon vegetable oil

¾ teaspoon salt, divided

3 cups torn kale leaves

1 large sweet potato

2 medium Yukon gold potatoes

2 to 3 tablespoons water

½ teaspoon garlic powder

¼ teaspoon freshly ground black pepper

I sometimes feel sad for tempeh because I think it's one of the most overlooked vegan proteins—which is crazy, because it's so versatile, and the texture (when cooked correctly) is fabulous. I love a good sweet 'n' spicy combo, and the maple syrup and Sriracha in this dish really deliver, especially with the hearty, toothsome tempeh. I also like how simple the potato base of this bowl is—just salt and pepper and garlic—so your taste buds can really focus on the maple-Sriracha flavor. #TeamTempeh

1. In a medium bowl, stir together the maple syrup and Sriracha. Add the tempeh and stir well to coat. Let sit for at least 15 minutes.

2. In a skillet over medium-high heat, heat the vegetable oil until it shimmers.

3. Using a slotted spoon, scoop the tempeh out of the marinade (reserving the sauce and bowl) and put it into the skillet. Cook, without stirring, for 3 to 4 minutes, or until it's crispy and brown on one side. Flip the pieces over and cook for 2 to 3 minutes more, until crispy and brown. Remove the skillet from the heat, and stir in ¼ teaspoon of salt, the reserved sauce, and the kale. Transfer the tempeh and kale mixture back into the marinade bowl.

4. Spiralize the sweet potato and Yukon gold potatoes using the Angel Hair blade and trim the spirals to 5- to 6-inch lengths.

5. Return the skillet to medium heat, and add the water to deglaze the pan, scraping up any browned bits from the bottom with a wooden spoon.

6. Add the sweet potato and potato spirals, the remaining ½ teaspoon of salt, garlic powder, and pepper. Sauté for 5 to 7 minutes, or until soft.

7. To serve, top the potato noodles with the tempeh and kale mixture (you may have to reheat it).

Serving tip: Want extra heat? Drizzle hot sauce over the bowls before serving!

Per serving: Calories: 326; Total fat: 10g; Total carbs: 49g; Fiber: 4g; Sugar: 14g; Protein: 14g; Sodium: 543mg

Roasted Buffalo Cauliflower Bowl

SERVES 4

Prep time: 15 minutes
Cook time: 40 minutes

Nonstick cooking spray

1 head cauliflower, chopped into florets

¾ cup Buffalo sauce, divided

1 large sweet potato

4 large carrots

2 tablespoons water

1 tablespoon nutritional yeast

½ teaspoon salt

⅛ teaspoon freshly ground black pepper

Vegan ranch dressing, for topping (optional)

Vegan blue cheese dressing, for topping (optional)

Chopped fresh basil, for topping (optional)

Diced celery, for topping (optional)

Diced bell peppers, any color, for topping (optional)

When you order Buffalo wings, they're usually served with carrots and celery on the side. Now the carrots are underneath! And they're noodles! As crazy as that may sound, I think you should go crazier still with the toppings.

1. Preheat the oven to 375°F. Coat a baking sheet with cooking spray.

2. In a large bowl, toss together the cauliflower florets and ½ cup of Buffalo sauce. Spread the cauliflower in a single layer on the prepared baking sheet and bake for 30 to 40 minutes, stirring once. The florets are done when they are lightly browned and slightly toasted.

3. While the cauliflower bakes, spiralize the sweet potato and carrots using the Fine Shred blade.

4. In a large skillet over medium heat, heat the water. Add the sweet potato and carrot spirals and sauté for 5 to 7 minutes, or until just barely soft. Season the vegetables with the nutritional yeast, salt, and pepper.

5. Divide the vegetables into four bowls, and top each with the roasted cauliflower. Drizzle with the remaining ¼ cup of Buffalo sauce. Add toppings, as desired.

Per serving: Calories: 127; Total fat: 1g; Total carbs: 27g; Fiber: 9g; Sugar: 10g; Protein: 7g; Sodium: 394mg

Snacks + Sides

Garlicky Sage Oven Fries, page 59

Baked Cinnamon-Apple Curls

SERVES 4 TO 6
Prep time: 10 minutes
Cook time: 1 hour,
30 minutes

3 medium apples (sweet
or tart varieties work best)

1½ teaspoons ground
cinnamon

½ teaspoon sugar

Pinch salt

Apples make the perfect snack, especially when you get a little creative. These Baked Cinnamon-Apple Curls are just a tiny bit sweet and perfect for on the go. Cinnamon is my favorite flavor, but to keep your snackers from getting bored, you can also try pumpkin spice or even Chinese five-spice powder! The important thing is to make sure all the apple slices are the same thickness so they bake evenly.

1. Preheat the oven to 250°F. Line a large baking sheet with parchment paper.

2. Spiralize the apples using the Coarse Wavy blade and trim the spirals into individual rings.

3. In a large bowl, stir together the cinnamon, sugar, and salt. Add the apples and toss until evenly coated. Place the rings in a single layer on the prepared baking sheet (use multiple baking sheets if necessary).

4. Bake for 50 to 60 minutes, or until the edges are dried and starting to curl slightly. If the apples are crisp, they're done. If they're not quite crisp, flip them with a spatula and cook for 10 to 20 minutes more.

5. Remove them from the oven and let cool. These will keep, refrigerated in an airtight container, for 3 to 4 days.

Per serving: Calories: 97; Total fat: 0g; Total carbs: 26g; Fiber: 6g; Sugar: 18g; Protein: 1g; Sodium: 41mg

Hummus Bites

SERVES 4
Prep time: 15 minutes
Cook time: 55 minutes

Nonstick cooking spray

1 large sweet potato

2 tablespoons
chickpea flour

¼ teaspoon salt

⅛ teaspoon freshly
ground black pepper

½ vegan egg (my favorites
are Follow Your Heart
and Just)

¼ cup hummus

Fresh herbs, for topping

Hot sauce, for topping

If you love throwing a party as much as I do, then this recipe is going to scream *HORS D'OEUVRES* at you. Build these bites on a beautiful serving tray, as they make a great appetizer. They also make an excellent snack for movie night on the couch, or even a light lunch.

1. Preheat the oven to 365°F. Coat a 12-cup muffin tin with cooking spray (or use a silicone pan). Set aside.

2. Bring a large saucepan of water to a boil over high heat.

3. Spiralize the sweet potato using the Angel Hair blade and trim the spirals to 3- to 4-inch lengths. Add the spirals to the boiling water, reduce the heat to maintain a simmer, and cook for 5 minutes. Drain and let the spirals sit in the pan for a minute or so, stirring, to get rid of any excess liquid.

4. Add the flour, salt, pepper, and egg to the pot, and mix well. Evenly divide the mixture among the prepared muffin cups, pressing down hard with the back of a spoon. Bake for 45 to 50 minutes, or until they're firm.

5. Let cool for about 5 minutes before popping them out of the pan and placing on a wire rack to cool.

6. Plate the sweet potato bites, and top each with about 1 teaspoon of hummus. Sprinkle with herbs and hot sauce, as desired, and serve.

Per serving: Calories: 70; Total fat: 2g; Total carbs: 11g; Fiber: 3g; Sugar: 2g; Protein: 3g; Sodium: 210mg

Spicy Southwestern Parsnip Fries

SERVES 4

Prep time: 10 minutes

Cook time: 25 minutes

Nonstick cooking spray

8 large parsnips

3 tablespoons olive oil

½ to 1 teaspoon salt

½ to 1 teaspoon chili powder

½ teaspoon garlic powder

½ teaspoon ground cumin

½ teaspoon onion powder

¼ teaspoon smoked paprika

¼ teaspoon freshly ground black pepper

Ranch Dressing (page 175), for dipping

These are what I make when I'm craving fries but feeling potato-ed out, or when I'm cooking for someone else and want to impress them with my fancy fry game. Parsnips are great to begin with, but I love them with this Southwestern spicy flavor. Short on time or spices? Using a premade taco-style spice mix is completely acceptable.

1. Preheat the oven to 350°F. Lightly coat a baking sheet with cooking spray.

2. Spiralize the parsnips using the Curly Fry blade and transfer to a large bowl.

3. Add the olive oil, salt, chili powder, garlic powder, cumin, onion powder, paprika, and pepper. Toss until coated.

4. Spread the fries on the prepared baking sheet, being careful not to crowd or layer them. Bake for 20 to 25 minutes, flipping them after 10 minutes, until crisp and lightly golden.

Ingredient tip: Parsnips have a nutty, slightly sweet flavor and are a fantastic source of vitamins C and K.

Per serving: Calories: 294; Total fat: 11g; Total carbs: 49g; Fiber: 13g; Sugar: 13g; Protein: 3g; Sodium: 265mg

Garlicky Sage Oven Fries

SERVES 4
Prep time: 40 minutes
Cook time: 30 minutes

2 large, or 3 medium,
russet potatoes

1½ tablespoons olive oil

2 garlic cloves, minced

14 fresh sage leaves,
roughly diced

1 teaspoon salt, plus more
for seasoning

¼ teaspoon freshly ground
black pepper, plus more
for seasoning

In my daydreams, I have a garden full of fresh herbs just outside my kitchen. When I'm cooking and need something, I just pop outside to grab a few leaves, and I'm set. In reality, this is never going to happen (I have a black thumb and a terrible memory, so the poor herbs would never get watered), but if by some miracle, there were sage growing just outside my door, I'd be making these fries all the darn time!

1. Spiralize the potatoes using the Curly Fry blade and trim the spirals to 5- to 6-inch lengths. Put the spirals in a large bowl, cover with cold water, and let soak for 30 minutes. Drain and completely dry the potatoes, and return them to the bowl.

2. Preheat the oven to 425°F.

3. In a small bowl, whisk together the olive oil, garlic, sage, salt, and pepper until combined. Pour the mixture over the potatoes and toss to coat. Spread the potatoes on a baking sheet, making sure not to crowd or layer them. Bake for 25 to 30 minutes, or until browned and crispy.

4. Season to taste with more salt and pepper.

Preparation tip: If some of the curly fries are baking faster than others, remove them from the baking sheet so they don't burn. Just mix them all back in again before adding the seasoning with salt and pepper.

Per serving: Calories: 295; Total fat: 19g; Total carbs: 30g; Fiber: 5g; Sugar: 2g; Protein: 3g; Sodium: 593mg

Salt-and-Pepper Summer Squash

SERVES 4

Prep time: 5 minutes
Cook time: 18 minutes

2 small to medium
summer squash

2 tablespoons vegan
butter, divided

¼ to ½ teaspoon salt

⅛ teaspoon freshly
ground black pepper

I grew up eating a version of these, where the squash was simply cut into thin rounds. It's actually the only thing I can remember my stepfather ever cooking for us, and I'm pretty sure it was always an impromptu snack, never part of a meal. And, honestly, this is how I still eat them most of the time! They're so much fancier as spirals than circles, though, so they'd make an excellent side dish.

1. Spiralize the squash using the Curly Fry blade and trim the spirals to 3- to 4-inch lengths.

2. In a large skillet over medium-high heat, melt 1 tablespoon of butter.

3. When the butter starts to bubble, add the summer squash in a single layer. Depending on how large your skillet is, you may need to cook the squash in two batches. Press the squash down with a spatula and cook for about 5 minutes, without stirring, until it starts to lightly brown. Sprinkle half the salt and pepper, stir, and cook for 1 to 2 minutes more, until evenly browned.

4. If needed, remove the squash from the pan and repeat with the second batch, using the remaining 1 tablespoon of butter and remaining salt and pepper. When done, return the first batch to the skillet to rewarm the squash before serving.

Per serving: Calories: 66; Total fat: 6g; Total carbs: 3g; Fiber: 1g; Sugar: 2g; Protein: 1g; Sodium: 367mg

Pan-Fried Sweet Potato Noodles

SERVES 4

Prep time: 10 minutes

Cook time: 15 minutes

1 large sweet potato

2 to 3 tablespoons water

1 tablespoon vegetable oil

½ sweet or white onion, diced

1 garlic clove, minced

3 tablespoons lite soy sauce, plus more for topping

⅔ cup frozen peas

½ teaspoon ground ginger

Sliced scallions (green parts only), for topping

Wilted bok choy, for topping

These pan-fried noodles are an excellent way to get that takeout fix without leaving the house. I recommend using oil instead of water to finish sautéing: It gets the noodles crispy.

1. Spiralize the sweet potato using the Coarse Shred blade and trim the spirals to 4- to 5-inch lengths.

2. In a large skillet over medium-high heat, heat the water. Add the sweet potato spirals and sauté for 3 to 4 minutes. Remove the sweet potatoes from the pan and set aside.

3. Return the skillet to medium-high heat, and heat the vegetable oil until it shimmers.

4. Add the onion and cook for 1 to 2 minutes, stirring as needed. Add the garlic and cook for 1 to 2 minutes more, still stirring, until fragrant.

5. Reduce the heat to medium-low, and add the sweet potatoes, soy sauce, peas, and ginger. Use the back of a spoon to press down everything and cook, without stirring, for 4 to 5 minutes. You'll know it's ready when the sweet potato noodles are crispy.

6. Stir and make sure everything is warmed through. Top with more soy sauce, sliced scallions, and bok choy, as desired.

Per serving: Calories: 89; Total fat: 4g; Total carbs: 13g; Fiber: 3g; Sugar: 4g; Protein: 3g; Sodium: 643mg

Creamy Coleslaw

SERVES 4

Prep time: 15 minutes, plus 30 minutes to chill

For the dressing

¾ cup vegan mayonnaise

3 tablespoons sugar

1½ tablespoons apple cider vinegar

½ teaspoon salt

freshly ground black pepper

For the slaw

1 small head green cabbage (or half a large head)

½ sweet onion

1 medium to large carrot

Salt

Freshly ground black pepper

Coleslaw has always been my barbecue side of choice. It was one of the things I missed most when I first went vegan. There's a barbecue joint near my mom's place that makes a mean barbecue tofu sandwich, but their coleslaw isn't vegan, so I always feel like I'm missing out. Would it be weird to bring a batch with me?

To make the dressing

In a medium bowl, whisk together the mayonnaise, sugar, vinegar, salt, and pepper until smooth and combined. Set aside.

To make the slaw

1. Spiralize the cabbage and onion using the Flat blade.

2. Spiralize the carrot using the Fine Shred blade.

3. On a clean work surface or cutting board, roughly chop the cabbage and carrot spirals so none of the pieces are too long. Chop the onion spirals a little bit finer as well (I prefer to keep them about half the length of the other veggies).

4. In a large bowl, combine the cabbage, onion, carrot, and dressing, and stir well to combine. Season to taste with salt and pepper. Refrigerate for at least 30 minutes before serving.

Serving tip: Serve with the Barbecue Tofu Bowl (page 36) or the Jerk Tofu Sandwiches (page 72)!

Per serving: Calories: 196; Total fat: 11g; Total carbs: 25g; Fiber: 5g; Sugar: 16g; Protein: 3g; Sodium: 811mg

Wasabi Potato Salad

SERVES 4 TO 6
Prep time: 15 minutes
Cook time: 7 minutes

2 white sweet potatoes

2 to 3 tablespoons water

1 large carrot

1 small jicama (about the size of an apple), rind removed

½ small cucumber

½ cup vegan mayonnaise, plus more as needed

1½ tablespoons Dijon mustard

1 to 3 teaspoons wasabi paste

½ teaspoon salt, plus more as needed

⅛ to ¼ teaspoon freshly ground black pepper, plus more as needed

This potato salad has sweet potatoes and wasabi for a magical flavor combination. I like using white sweet potatoes, so no one suspects that hint of sweetness when they take their first bite . . . and then they get that wasabi heat! Bring this version of potato salad to your next barbecue and accept all the praise you're sure to get, then send me a thank-you card. You're welcome.

1. Spiralize the sweet potatoes using the Curly Fry blade and trim the spirals to 2- to 3-inch lengths.

2. In a large skillet over medium-high heat, heat the water. Add the sweet potato spirals and sauté for 5 to 7 minutes, or until soft. Transfer to a large bowl and let cool.

3. Spiralize the carrot, jicama, and cucumber using the Fine Shred blade and trim the spirals to 2- to 3-inch lengths. Using a paper towel, squeeze the excess liquid from the cucumber and jicama, and add them and the carrot to the sweet potatoes.

4. In a small bowl, whisk together the mayonnaise, mustard, wasabi paste, salt, and pepper. Add the mixture to the vegetables, and gently stir to combine and coat. Season to taste with more salt and pepper, or add more mayonnaise if you want a creamier salad. Serve chilled.

Preparation tip: Sweet potato noodles are too delicate to boil, which is why we water-sauté them.

Per serving: Calories: 190; Total fat: 9g; Total carbs: 27g; Fiber: 7g; Sugar: 6g; Protein: 2g; Sodium: 564mg

Balsamic Roasted Carrots

SERVES 4

Prep time: 10 minutes

Cook time: 30 minutes

2 tablespoons olive oil

2 tablespoons balsamic vinegar

¼ to ½ teaspoon garlic salt, plus more as needed

⅛ teaspoon freshly ground black pepper

8 to 10 large carrots

Where roasting brings out the natural sweetness of the carrots, the balsamic vinegar gives it a nice bite. These are great as part of a rich meal to add something light or as a side dish at your next backyard barbecue!

1. Preheat the oven to 350°F. Line a baking sheet with parchment paper.

2. In a large bowl, whisk together the olive oil, vinegar, garlic salt, and pepper until combined.

3. Spiralize the carrots using the Coarse Wave blade and toss them in the vinegar mixture to coat. Pour the carrots onto the prepared baking sheet and bake for 25 to 30 minutes, flipping once halfway through the baking time. They're done when they're browned and just a little crispy.

4. Season to taste with more garlic salt.

Per serving: Calories: 137; Total fat: 7g; Total carbs: 18g; Fiber: 5g; Sugar: 9g; Protein: 2g; Sodium: 124mg

Potatoes au Gratin

SERVES 4 TO 6
Prep time: 15 minutes
Cook time: 1 hour,
10 minutes

Nonstick cooking spray

2 tablespoons vegan
butter

1 small sweet onion,
roughly diced

2 garlic cloves, minced

2½ tablespoons flour

1 cup unsweetened
cashew milk

1¼ cups vegan cheddar
shreds, divided

½ to 1 teaspoon sea salt

¼ teaspoon freshly ground
black pepper

⅛ teaspoon chili powder

2 small Yukon gold
potatoes

1 medium sweet potato

½ cup panko bread
crumbs

You learn a lot when you write a cookbook . . . mostly about yourself and how little sleep you actually need. In this case, I also (finally) learned the difference between scalloped potatoes and potatoes au gratin. Basically, the difference is cheese. These potatoes have lots of gooey, melted, delicious vegan cheese, so they are "au gratin." I prefer to keep the skins on my potatoes for the extra fiber and nutrients, but if you want a more polished look, peel them.

1. Preheat the oven to 350°F. Lightly coat a 1½-quart baking dish with cooking spray.

2. In a medium skillet over medium-high heat, melt the butter.

3. Add the onion and sauté for 2 to 3 minutes.

4. Add the garlic and sauté for 1 to 2 minutes more, or until fragrant.

5. Stir in the flour and cook for 2 minutes, making sure everything is mixed well.

6. Stir in the milk and reduce the heat to low. Cook, stirring frequently, for about 2 minutes, until the sauce thickens.

7. Stir in 1 cup of cheddar shreds, as well as the sea salt, black pepper, and chili powder, and turn off the heat.

CONTINUED

8. Spiralize the potatoes and sweet potato using the Flat blade and arrange them in the prepared baking dish. (Mix them up or layer them by color—have fun with this!) Pour the cheese sauce over the top, and use a spoon to press down on the potatoes.

9. Top with the remaining ¼ cup of cheddar shreds and the bread crumbs. Spritz the bread crumbs with cooking spray, and cover the dish with foil.

10. Bake for 60 to 65 minutes, or until the potatoes are soft. The sweet potatoes take a minute or two longer than the Yukons, so be sure to test both. You can also remove the foil and put the dish in the broiler on low for 30 to 60 seconds, if you want a browner top.

Substitution tip: I used cheddar shreds, but you can change up the flavor profile by mixing in some pepper Jack, or even a smoked Gouda.

Per serving: Calories: 350; Total fat: 15g; Total carbs: 48g; Fiber: 6g; Sugar: 4g; Protein: 6g; Sodium: 584mg

Sandwiches + Wraps

Sweet 'n' Spicy Beet Wraps, page 79

Fried Teriyaki Tempeh Sandwiches

SERVES 4

Prep time: 10 minutes, plus 15 to 30 minutes to marinate tempeh
Cook time: 10 minutes

1 (8-ounce) package tempeh, cut into 8 thin rectangles

½ cup teriyaki sauce

1 green bell pepper

½ small to medium sweet potato

1 tablespoon avocado oil

8 slices bread, toasted

1 avocado, halved, pitted, and lightly mashed

¼ teaspoon garlic salt

Sticky, sweet teriyaki tempeh and crisp, fresh veggies make amazing sandwich partners! Especially with the creamy avocado slathered on the toasted bread. No one flavor is overwhelming—instead, they work together in perfect unison. This sandwich may take a little more effort to put together than one made with your average cold cuts, but it's worth it!

1. In a medium shallow bowl, combine the tempeh and teriyaki sauce. Set aside to marinate for 15 to 30 minutes, depending on how much time you have.

2. While the tempeh marinates, spiralize the green bell pepper and sweet potato using the Angel Hair blade, and trim the sweet potato spirals to 1- to 2-inch lengths. Set aside.

3. In a large skillet over medium heat, heat the avocado oil until it shimmers.

4. Add the tempeh slices (reserve the marinade). Cook, without moving the slices, for 3 to 4 minutes, or until golden brown. Flip and cook the other side until golden.

5. Slather each slice of toast with avocado and sprinkle with garlic salt. Add two slices of tempeh to each sandwich, and top with the raw green bell pepper and the sweet potato spirals.

6. Drizzle each sandwich with 1 to 2 teaspoons of the reserved marinade before topping with the remaining toast slices.

Ingredient tip: If you don't have avocado oil on hand, use a mild vegetable oil instead. You don't want anything that will overpower the other flavors in this sandwich.

Per serving: Calories: 375; Total fat: 15g; Total carbs: 46g; Fiber: 5g; Sugar: 9g; Protein: 18g; Sodium: 1432mg

Jerk Tofu Sandwiches

SERVES 4

Prep time: 15 minutes, plus 30 minutes to marinate the tofu

Cook time: 18 minutes

For the tofu

4 tablespoons jerk seasoning, divided

1 ½ to 2 tablespoons vegetable oil, divided

1 tablespoon lite soy sauce

1 tablespoon pure maple syrup

1 (14-ounce) block firm tofu, drained, pressed for at least one hour, and cut into 8 thin rectangles

For the sandwiches

Nonstick cooking spray

4 pineapple rings

2 tablespoons vegan mayonnaise

8 slices bread, lightly toasted

½ batch Creamy Coleslaw (page 62) with 2 teaspoons freshly squeezed lime juice mixed in

I love a good sandwich, and this one is even more fun when paired with a side of pineapple. Or sweet potato fries sprinkled with jerk seasoning! Make sure to pair this recipe with an extra napkin, because things do get a little messy. My favorite part of this dish is how sticky and flavorful the tofu gets after being pan-fried. Definitely a good way to serve tofu to someone who isn't convinced they're going to like it!

To make the tofu

1. In a shallow baking dish, stir together the jerk seasoning, 1 tablespoon of vegetable oil, soy sauce, and maple syrup.

2. Lay the tofu pieces in the marinade and let sit for 30 minutes, flipping if necessary for complete coverage.

3. In a large skillet over medium-high heat, heat the remaining vegetable oil until it shimmers.

4. Add the tofu slices (reserve the marinade) in a single layer and drizzle 1 teaspoon or so of the marinade over them. Cook for 6 to 8 minutes per side, or until crispy and golden brown. Drizzle more marinade over the top after you flip them, and again when they're about 1 minute from being done. The marinade cooks down and makes the tofu sticky and delicious!

5. Remove the tofu from the skillet and set aside.

1. Return the skillet to the heat and add a spritz of cooking spray. Place the pineapple rings in the skillet, and cook for about 1 minute on each side—you want them to grab some of the marinade flavor and brown a tiny bit; we're not trying to cook them. Remove the pineapple from the skillet.

2. Spread a small amount of mayonnaise on four slices of bread. Place two slices of tofu on each, and top with a pineapple ring and a drizzle of marinade. Spoon on a couple tablespoons of coleslaw and top with the remaining pieces of bread.

Serving tip: Have extra coleslaw? Use a small amount to replace the mayonnaise on the bottom slice of bread, or serve it as a side.

Per serving: Calories: 462; Total fat: 19g; Total carbs: 66g; Fiber: 7g; Sugar: 30g; Protein: 15g; Sodium: 905mg

Hummus Veggie Lettuce Wraps

SERVES 4

Prep time: 15 minutes

3 large carrots

1 small sweet potato

1 bell pepper, any color

½ small cucumber

8 large Boston lettuce leaves

1½ to 2 cups hummus

¼ teaspoon salt

Thinly sliced scallions (green parts only), for topping (optional)

Red pepper flakes, for topping (optional)

Hot sauce, for topping (optional)

I like to call these Dip in a Wrap because I took the veggies you usually dip into hummus, spiralized them, and wrapped them up! I'll have these wraps as a light lunch when I'm working around the house and don't want a heavy meal weighing me down. I recommend using hummus with a lot of flavor—maybe roasted red pepper, garlic, or even beet! This recipe makes eight wraps, but they're really light, so I consider it to be four servings.

1. Spiralize the carrots, sweet potato, bell pepper, and cucumber using the Angel Hair blade.

2. Place the lettuce leaves on a clean work surface and fill each with hummus, using a spoon to smooth it out evenly.

3. Top each with a mixture of the vegetables, and season with salt.

4. Add any additional toppings, as desired, and serve slightly chilled.

Ingredient tip: Boston and butter lettuce are practically the same, with a very similar appearance and taste, so you can use either. Bibb lettuce is also similar, but it's smaller and will hold less filling.

Per serving: Calories: 277; Total fat: 12g; Total carbs: 34g; Fiber: 11g; Sugar: 7g; Protein: 12g; Sodium: 549mg

Spicy Veggie Pita Wraps

SERVES 4

Prep time: 15 minutes

For the spicy sauce

½ cup vegan mayonnaise

1 tablespoon Sriracha

2 teaspoons freshly squeezed lime juice

¼ teaspoon red pepper flakes

Pinch salt

Pinch freshly ground black pepper

For the wraps

2 green bell peppers

1 medium sweet potato

½ cucumber

Salt

Freshly ground black pepper

4 whole-grain pita breads

1 heaping cup chopped lettuce

1 medium tomato, diced

Ranch Dressing (page 175), for topping (optional)

Sriracha, for topping (optional)

In case you couldn't tell by the recipe name, these wraps are spicy. If you find them a little too spicy, schmear some avocado, or even just some plain vegan mayo, on your pita bread. Personally, I like the heat; it makes them a little more fun than your average veggie wrap. I also purposely keep all the veggies raw to make it light and healthy. Because they're spiralized so thinly, they really don't need to be cooked.

To make the spicy sauce

In a large bowl, whisk together the mayonnaise, Sriracha, lime juice, red pepper flakes, salt, and pepper. Taste. Not spicy enough? Stir in more Sriracha!

To make the wraps

1. Spiralize the green bell peppers, sweet potato, and cucumber using the Angel Hair blade. Using a paper towel, gently squeeze out the excess liquid. Add all the spirals to the spicy sauce and toss until fully coated. Season to taste with salt and pepper.

2. Top the pitas with the spiraled veggies, lettuce, and tomato.

3. Drizzle with the Ranch Dressing (if using, but the meal won't be nut free) and more Sriracha (if using) before wrapping and eating.

Per serving: Calories: 211; Total fat: 8g; Total carbs: 33g; Fiber: 5g; Sugar: 6g; Protein: 5g; Sodium: 547mg

Cheesy Barbecue Collard Wraps

MAKES 6 WRAPS

Prep time: 15 minutes

Cook time: 18 minutes

6 large collard green leaves, rinsed well and dried

1 medium head cauliflower

1 tablespoon olive oil

1 cup vegan cheddar shreds

¼ cup nondairy milk

½ to 1 teaspoon salt, plus more as needed

¼ teaspoon freshly ground black pepper, plus more as needed

¼ teaspoon garlic powder

1 small butternut squash

2 to 3 tablespoons water

3 to 4 tablespoons barbecue sauce

Gooey, cheesy sauce and barbecue *anything* go together really well. Don't you agree? I'm not proud of this, but I've been known to top bowls of mac 'n' cheese with barbecue sauce. It's just too good! What I like about these wraps is that using cauliflower rice instead of pasta and collard greens instead of a tortilla keeps this meal nice and light. Don't have collard greens? Bibb lettuce will also work; it's just a little less hearty.

1. Prep your collard leaves: Using a sharp paring knife, shave down the thick stems, cutting away the thickest parts so they are less bulky. Set aside.

2. Spiralize the cauliflower into rice using the Flat blade.

3. In a large skillet over medium heat, heat the olive oil until it shimmers.

4. Add the cauliflower rice and sauté for 4 to 5 minutes, stirring frequently, or until cooked.

5. Reduce the heat to low and stir in the cheddar, milk, salt, pepper, and garlic powder. Cover the skillet and cook for 2 to 3 minutes, stirring a couple of times, until the cheese melts completely. Remove the pan from the heat and set aside (you may need to reheat the cauliflower mixture before building the wraps).

6. Cut off the bulbous end of the butternut squash and reserve for another use. Trim the ends of the remaining neck piece and slice or peel off the rind. Spiralize the neck piece using the Fine Shred blade.

7. In another large skillet over medium-high heat, heat the water. Add the butternut squash spirals and sauté for 5 to 7 minutes, or until soft. Turn off the heat, drain any excess liquid, and stir in the barbecue sauce. Season to taste with salt and pepper.

8. Place the collard leaves on a clean work surface, and evenly divide the cheesy cauliflower rice and barbecue squash noodles among them, placing the filling near the top to middle part of each leaf. Fold and wrap the leaves as if you're making a burrito, and serve warm.

Ingredient tip: One cup of collard greens provides 21 percent of the calcium you need daily—more than any other vegetable!

Per serving: Calories: 188; Total fat: 7g; Total carbs: 30g; Fiber: 8g; Sugar: 7g; Protein: 6g; Sodium: 493mg

Creamy Avocado Squash Wraps

SERVES 4

Prep time: 15 minutes

1 small summer squash

1 small zucchini

1 red bell pepper

½ teaspoon salt, divided

⅛ teaspoon freshly ground black pepper

⅛ teaspoon chili powder

2 avocados, halved and pitted

1 teaspoon freshly squeezed lime juice

4 (9-inch) tortillas

1 cup Ranch Dressing (page 175)

Remember those cream cheese tortilla logs that everyone used to bring to potlucks (and maybe still do)? I wanted something evocative of that, but healthier—more veggies, please! Even though there are plenty of fantastic vegan cream cheeses on the market, I wanted to keep it a bit more "whole food."

1. Spiralize the squash, zucchini, and red bell pepper using the Fine Shred blade and trim the spirals to 3- to 4-inch lengths. Combine the spirals in a large bowl and sprinkle with ¼ teaspoon of salt, pepper, and chili powder. Stir well to coat.

2. Scoop the avocado flesh into a small bowl, add the lime juice and the remaining ¼ teaspoon of salt, and mash to combine.

3. Place the tortillas on a clean work surface and schmear each evenly with the avocado, leaving about a ¼-inch border around the edges.

4. Top each with the vegetable spirals, and drizzle each tortilla with ¼ cup of Ranch Dressing. Wrap as you would a burrito. Enjoy!

Per serving: Calories: 402; Total fat: 22g; Total carbs: 43g; Fiber: 10g; Sugar: 6g; Protein: 9g; Sodium: 743mg

Sweet 'n' Spicy Beet Wraps

MAKES 4 WRAPS
Prep time: 10 minutes
Cook time: 15 minutes

For the sauce

½ cup packed light brown sugar

2 tablespoons lite soy sauce

1 tablespoon hot sauce

2 teaspoons apple cider vinegar

For the wraps

Nonstick cooking spray

4 large beets

¼ teaspoon salt

⅛ teaspoon freshly ground black pepper

⅛ to ¼ teaspoon chili powder

4 whole-grain wraps or pita

1 avocado, halved, pitted, and lightly mashed

2 cups baby arugula

Please don't tell the other recipes in this book, but this one is my favorite. I'm a beet fangirl to begin with, but when they're roasted with a hint of chili powder, they reach a whole new level. Combined with sweet 'n' spicy sauce and cool, creamy avocado . . . this sandwich is perfection. I also love the bite from the baby arugula. Start with a small amount of chili powder on your beets, and taste before adding more!

To make the sauce

In a small bowl, whisk together the brown sugar, soy sauce, hot sauce, and vinegar. Set aside.

To make the wraps

1. Preheat the oven to 400°F. Coat a baking sheet with cooking spray.

2. Spiralize the beets using the Curly Fry blade and trim the spirals to 5- to 6-inch lengths. Spread the spirals in a single layer on the prepared baking sheet, and spritz with the cooking spray. Season with salt, pepper, and chili powder.

3. Bake for 15 minutes, stirring once about halfway through. They're done when just barely soft.

CONTINUED

4. Place the wraps on a clean work surface and schmear each with avocado. Top with the beets and arugula. Drizzle each with the sauce. Fold in half and enjoy!

Per serving: Calories: 438; Total fat: 13g; Total carbs: 74g; Fiber: 12g; Sugar: 38g; Protein: 9g; Sodium: 1253mg

Roasted Butternut Squash Wraps

SERVES 4

Prep time: 10 minutes
Cook time: 10 minutes

1 medium butternut squash

1 tablespoon olive oil

Salt

Freshly ground black pepper

4 whole-grain tortillas or flatbreads

¼ cup vegan mayonnaise

¼ teaspoon garlic powder

4 slices vegan cheddar cheese

1 cup baby lettuce leaves

When butternut squash goes on sale, I tend to buy a lot. Okay, maybe I buy them all. It's just that I love butternut squash, and they seem to keep forever, so it makes sense to stock up. If you, too, have a stack of squash on your kitchen counter, these wraps are an easy and yummy way to use up at least one.

1. Preheat the oven to 400°F.

2. Cut off the bulbous end of the butternut squash and reserve for another use. Trim the end of the remaining neck piece and slice or peel off the rind. Spiralize the neck piece using the Curly Fry blade and trim the spirals to 3- to 4-inch lengths. Put the spirals on a rimmed baking sheet, sprinkle with the olive oil, season with salt and pepper, and turn to coat. Arrange the squash noodles evenly.

3. Roast for 8 to 10 minutes, or until soft, stirring at least once about halfway through. Remove from the oven and set aside to cool.

4. Place the tortillas on a clean work surface and schmear each with mayonnaise. Sprinkle with garlic powder. Add the cheese and butternut squash. Top with the lettuce, and roll or fold to close.

Per serving: Calories: 400; Total fat: 18g; Total carbs: 55g; Fiber: 10g; Sugar: 5g; Protein: 9g; Sodium: 731mg

Spicy Thai Chickpea Burgers

SERVES 4
Prep time: 15 minutes, plus
30 minutes to chill
Cook time: 45 minutes

1 medium sweet potato

1 (15.5-ounce) can
chickpeas, rinsed and
drained

12 fresh basil leaves, plus
more for topping

2 to 3 tablespoons
sambal oelek

½ to 1 teaspoon salt

1 teaspoon freshly
squeezed lime juice

½ teaspoon ground ginger

4 scallions (green parts
only), thinly sliced

½ to 1 cup panko
bread crumbs

Nonstick cooking spray

4 burger buns

Lettuce leaves, for topping

Tomato slices, for topping

Vegan burgers that taste like the real deal dominate the world these days, but I still love a good old-fashioned bean burger, especially when it combines *sambal oelek* (Indonesian chili paste) and sweet basil. Know that bean burgers often fall apart when you eat them, but that's part of their charm! These are spicy but still very flavorful, so start with 2 tablespoons of *sambal oelek* and go from there. You can also load up on toppings—vegan mayo or cheese, avocado, sweet basil, more *sambal oelek*, or Thai sweet chili sauce are just some that come to mind!

1. Spiralize the sweet potato using the Angel Hair blade and trim the spirals to 2- to 3-inch lengths.

2. In a food processor, combine the chickpeas, basil, *sambal oelek*, salt, lime juice, and ginger. Blend until mostly smooth. Transfer to a large bowl, and add two-thirds of the sweet potato spirals and the scallions. Mixing by hand, add the bread crumbs slowly until you get a consistency you can shape into patties. Refrigerate the mix for at least 30 minutes, or longer if you can.

3. Preheat the oven to 400°F. Lightly coat a baking sheet with cooking spray.

4. Shape the chilled chickpea mix into four patties, and place them on the prepared baking sheet.

5. Bake for 35 to 45 minutes, flipping once about halfway through. If you want them a little browned, finish them in the broiler on low for 30 to 60 seconds, watching carefully.

6. When you build your burgers, use the remaining one-third of the sweet potato spirals as a slightly crispy topping, along with the lettuce, tomato, and whatever else your heart desires!

Serving tip: Looking for a way to use leftover chickpea burgers? I like to break mine up and use them as salad toppers!

Per serving: Calories: 405; Total fat: 6g; Total carbs: 74g; Fiber: 9g; Sugar: 7g; Protein: 15g; Sodium: 843mg

Beet Burgers

SERVES 4

Prep time: 20 minutes

Cook time: 22 minutes

3 medium beets

2 to 3 tablespoons water

1 (15.5-ounce) can chickpeas, rinsed and drained

3 to 4 fresh basil leaves

1 vegan egg (my favorites are Follow Your Heart and Just)

1 teaspoon freshly squeezed lemon juice

¾ cup quick-cooking oats

½ teaspoon salt, plus more as needed

¼ teaspoon garlic powder

1 tablespoon vegetable oil

4 burger buns

Lettuce leaves, for topping

Vegan cheese slices, for topping

Avocado slices, for topping

Beets are so good for us, and I include them in my diet as often as possible. This is a fairly recent obsession for me, though. I don't think I bought them at the store to cook until I was . . . 32? I was a late beet bloomer—but I've never looked back! Their sweet, earthy flavor works with all sorts of toppings.

1. Spiralize the beets using the Angel Hair blade and trim the spirals to 2 -to 3-inch lengths.

2. In a large skillet over medium-high heat, heat the water. Add the beet spirals and sauté for 5 to 7 minutes, or until soft. Remove from the skillet.

3. In a food processor, combine one-third of the spiraled beets, the chickpeas, basil, egg, lemon juice, oats, salt, and garlic powder. Pulse until well mixed. Add more salt to taste.

4. Remove the blade from the processor, and stir in another one-third of the spiraled beets. Use your hands to form the mixture into four patties.

5. In a large skillet over medium-high heat, heat the vegetable oil until it shimmers.

6. Add the patties and cook for 5 to 7 minutes per side, or until lightly browned and heated through.

7. Serve them on buns, topped with the remaining beet spirals and additional toppings, as desired.

Per serving: Calories: 524; Total fat: 17g; Total carbs: 80g; Fiber: 11g; Sugar: 8g; Protein: 15g; Sodium: 977mg

Soups + Salads

Sweet 'n' Spicy Fruit Salad, page 100

Veggie "Noodle" Soup with Chickpeas

SERVES 4

Prep time: 10 minutes
Cook time: 15 minutes

2 large carrots

1 small to medium sweet potato

2 to 3 tablespoons water

2 small sweet onions, diced

2 garlic cloves, minced

1 (15.5-ounce) can chickpeas, rinsed and drained

3 celery stalks, cut into ¼-inch-thick slices

2 dried whole bay leaves

½ teaspoon dried thyme

¼ teaspoon salt (unless you use a salty broth), plus more as needed

¼ teaspoon freshly ground black pepper, plus more as needed

3 cups vegetable broth

As I said, what I love about spiralizing isn't necessarily changing the way you eat; it's making the meals you eat a little different and a little more fun. This soup is a great example of that. It's the same basic ingredients and flavors you're used to in a veggie or chick'n noodle soup, but with veggies as the noodles instead of pasta!

1. Spiralize the carrots and sweet potato using the Angel Hair blade and trim the spirals to 1- to 2-lengths. Set aside.

2. In an 8-quart or larger stockpot over medium-high heat, heat the water. Add the onion and cook for 2 to 3 minutes.

3. Add the garlic and cook for 1 to 2 minutes, until fragrant.

4. Add the veggie spirals, chickpeas, celery, bay leaves, thyme, salt, pepper, and vegetable broth. Reduce the heat to maintain a simmer, and cook for 5 to 10 minutes, or until the soup is heated through and the vegetables are soft.

5. Remove and discard the bay leaves. Season to taste with salt and pepper.

Substitution tip: Use soy curls or any other mock chick'n product in place of chickpeas, if you prefer.

Per serving: Calories: 191; Total fat: 3g; Total carbs: 32g; Fiber: 8g; Sugar: 8g; Protein: 11g; Sodium: 679mg

Double Potato Cheddar Chowder

SERVES 4

Prep time: 15 minutes
Cook time: 17 minutes

4 medium Yukon gold potatoes

1 small to medium sweet potato

2 to 3 tablespoons water

2 celery stalks, cut into ¼-inch-thick slices

½ sweet onion, diced

2 cups unsweetened cashew milk, plus more as needed

1 cup vegetable broth

½ teaspoon salt

¼ teaspoon garlic powder

¼ teaspoon smoked paprika

⅛ to ¼ teaspoon freshly ground black pepper

1 cup frozen sweet corn kernels

1 cup vegan cheddar shreds

I'm not one of those vegans who shuns oil and vegan butter. At all. But I'm always happy to find ways to make my recipes a little healthier, as long as I don't lose any flavor. This chowder is one of those times! I skip the roux, so there's no butter or all-purpose flour in this chowder. Instead, the thickness comes from using your immersion blender. And if you're looking to spice things up, add ¼ to ½ cup roasted green chiles in step 4!

1. Spiralize the potatoes and sweet potato using the Curly Fry blade and trim the spirals to 1- to 2-inch lengths.

2. In an 8-quart or larger stockpot over medium-high heat, heat the water. Add the potato and sweet potato spirals, celery, and onion, and sauté for 5 to 6 minutes. When the potatoes are *almost* soft, remove the pot from the heat and drain any excess water. Stir in the cashew milk and vegetable broth.

3. Using an immersion blender on low speed for just a few moments, blend the soup until one-fourth to half the veggies are blended. Alternatively, if you don't have an immersion blender, transfer one-fourth to one-half of the soup to a standard blender and blend until smooth, then return the soup to the stockpot.

CONTINUED

4. Return the pot to medium-low heat, and stir in the salt, garlic powder, paprika, pepper, and corn. Simmer the soup, uncovered, for about 10 minutes, or until warmed through and the potatoes are fully cooked.

5. Stir in the cheese. Divide among four bowls and serve hot.

Ingredient tip: Smoked paprika is *very* different from the sweet version you may be used to. It has the most amazing flavor and is wonderful in dishes that traditionally contain ham, like a potato chowder.

Per serving: Calories: 231; Total fat: 8g; Total carbs: 35g; Fiber: 6g; Sugar: 4g; Protein: 5g; Sodium: 443mg

Creamy Garlic Zucchini Soup

SERVES 4

Prep time: 10 minutes
Cook time: 25 minutes

2 medium to large
zucchini

3 tablespoons vegan
butter

3 garlic cloves, minced

3 tablespoons all-purpose
flour

¼ teaspoon onion powder

2 cups unsweetened
nondairy milk

1 cup vegetable broth

¼ teaspoon salt, plus
more as needed

⅛ teaspoon freshly
ground black pepper, plus
more as needed

1 cup vegan cheddar
shreds

This soup is great for cold winter nights, but where I live in Colorado, we also get crazy thunderstorms in the summer. The sky gets dark and the temperature drops, and this soup is perfect for those nights, too.

1. Spiralize the zucchini using the Curly Fry blade and trim the spirals to 1- to 2-inch lengths. Set aside.

2. In an 8-quart or larger stockpot over medium-high heat, melt the butter until it bubbles.

3. Add the garlic and sauté, stirring, for 1 to 2 minutes, or until fragrant.

4. Stir in the flour and onion powder, and cook, stirring, for 2 to 3 minutes more until thick.

5. Whisk in the milk, vegetable broth, salt, and pepper, whisking until the roux is completely absorbed. Reduce the heat and simmer until the broth begins to thicken, 3 to 4 minutes.

6. Stir in the zucchini and simmer for 10 minutes, stirring every few minutes, gently, so as not to break up the zoodles, until the zucchini is soft.

CONTINUED

7. Add the cheddar shreds and remove the pot from the heat. Cover the pot and let sit for 1 to 2 minutes, until the cheese melts. Season to taste with salt and pepper.

Substitution tip: Substitute butternut squash or summer squash for zucchini.

Per serving: Calories: 209; Total fat: 14g; Total carbs: 16g; Fiber: 2g; Sugar: 2g; Protein: 4g; Sodium: 561mg

Plantain and Black Bean Soup

SERVES 4

Prep time: 15 minutes

Cook time: 25 minutes

1 tablespoon vegetable oil

1 small to medium sweet onion, diced

2 garlic cloves, minced

1 medium to large plantain, mostly green in color

2 cups vegetable broth

1 teaspoon paprika

½ teaspoon ground ginger

¼ teaspoon ground turmeric

¼ to ½ teaspoon salt

1 (14-ounce) can black beans, rinsed and drained

2 to 3 scallions (green parts only), thinly sliced

This is my version of a stew I had in Puerto Rico in 2017. All I had to base it on was a picture and my memories, so I'm not sure how authentic it is, but it's really, really yummy. Every time I taste it, I'm immediately transported back to that small café on a side street in San Juan. The spices and the plantain are such an easy way to recreate that little piece of paradise.

1. In a large skillet over medium-high heat, heat the vegetable oil until it shimmers.

2. Add the onion and sauté for 3 to 4 minutes.

3. Add the garlic and cook for 1 to 2 minutes more, or until fragrant.

4. Spiralize the plantain using the Angel Hair blade, and trim the spirals to 1- to 2-inch lengths. Add the plantain spirals to the skillet and gently stir in the vegetable broth, paprika, ginger, turmeric, and salt. Reduce the heat to low, cover the skillet, and simmer for 15 minutes.

5. Stir in the black beans and simmer for 5 minutes more.

6. Serve topped with the scallions.

Serving tip: Serve this soup with brown rice (or your favorite grain) to make it heartier or to stretch it further.

Per serving: Calories: 207; Total fat: 5g; Total carbs: 34g; Fiber: 8g; Sugar: 9g; Protein: 9g; Sodium: 534mg

Crispy Tofu Ramen

SERVES 4
Prep time: 15 minutes
Cook time: 15 minutes

For the crispy tofu

2 to 3 tablespoons vegetable oil

1 (14-ounce) package firm tofu, drained, pressed well, and cubed

¼ cup hoisin sauce

1 teaspoon Sriracha

Ramen is so comforting, and even though this is a hot soup, I still find myself craving it in the warm summer months. Thankfully, it's fairly quick and easy to whip up on the stovetop, so there's no need to heat up the kitchen too much. The crispy tofu is easily my favorite part of this recipe. Is there anything better than perfectly flavored tofu that is crisp on the outside and soft and pillowy on the inside? When it's paired with this flavorful broth, I'll say no, there's not!

To make the crispy tofu

1. In a large nonstick skillet over medium-high heat, heat 2 tablespoons of vegetable oil until it shimmers.

2. Add the tofu and cook until crispy and lightly browned, 2 to 3 minutes per side.

3. Pour in the hoisin and Sriracha, and stir the tofu to coat. Reduce the heat to low and simmer for 2 to 3 minutes. Remove from the heat.

To make the ramen

1. Cook the ramen noodles according to the package instructions. Drain and rinse with cold water. Set aside.

2. Spiralize the sweet potato using the Angel Hair blade.

3. In an 8-quart or larger stockpot over medium-high heat, heat the vegetable oil until it shimmers.

For the ramen

4 ounces dried ramen noodles

1 large sweet potato

2 tablespoons vegetable oil

3 garlic cloves, minced

1 (2-inch) piece fresh ginger, peeled and finely diced

2½ cups sliced shiitake mushrooms

4 scallions, roughly chopped

4 cups vegetable broth

2 tablespoons soy sauce

1 tablespoon miso paste

¼ teaspoon salt

Sriracha, for topping

Hoisin sauce, for topping

4. Add the garlic and ginger and sauté for 2 to 3 minutes, stirring frequently.

5. Add the sweet potato spirals and cook for 5 to 6 minutes, stirring frequently.

6. Add the mushrooms and scallions and cook for 2 minutes more.

7. Stir in the vegetable broth, soy sauce, miso, salt, and the cooked ramen noodles. Bring to a boil, cooking for just 1 minute. Serve hot, with the Sriracha and hoisin sauce for topping.

Ingredient tip: Did you know most soy sauce brands contain gluten? It's true! Check your local grocer for alternative brands when preparing this ramen for your gluten-free friends and family.

Per serving: Calories: 351; Total fat: 21g; Total carbs: 25g; Fiber: 4g; Sugar: 8g; Protein: 17g; Sodium: 1761mg

Three-Alarm Chili with Millet

SERVES 4

Prep time: 10 minutes
Cook time: 25 minutes

1 small sweet potato

1 small to medium zucchini

2 to 3 tablespoons water

1 sweet onion, diced

3 garlic cloves, minced

1 poblano pepper, diced

1 jalapeño pepper, diced

1 (15-ounce) can roasted diced tomatoes and their juices

1 (15-ounce) can red kidney beans, drained but not rinsed

1 teaspoon ground cumin

½ teaspoon salt

½ teaspoon smoked paprika

¼ teaspoon chili powder, plus more if you want it spicier

Chili is such a universal dish, perfect for so many occasions! Winter storm? Make chili. Football game? Make chili. I also really like it because it reheats so well (and with more flavor), so it's ideal for Sunday meal prep for work lunches. This chili is a little different than others because it's all about the (spiralized) veggies. I hope you'll enjoy it. Don't skip the smoked paprika—it's an important part of the overall flavor!

1. Spiralize the sweet potato and zucchini using the Coarse Shred blade and trim the spirals to 3- to 4-inch lengths. Set the zucchini aside.

2. In a large nonstick pot over medium heat, heat the water. Add the sweet potato spirals, onion, garlic, and peppers. Sauté for 3 to 4 minutes, adding more water, if needed.

3. Stir in the zucchini spirals, tomatoes, kidney beans, cumin, salt, paprika, and chili powder. Reduce the heat to maintain a simmer, and cook for 15 to 20 minutes.

4. To assemble your bowls, start with a layer of millet and top with the spinach. Add the chili last, the heat of which will soften the spinach. Add any additional toppings you like, and serve hot!

2 cups cooked millet

2 cups torn fresh baby
spinach leaves

Vegan sour cream,
for topping

Vegan cheddar shreds,
for topping

Chopped onion,
for topping

Red pepper flakes,
for topping

Preparation tip: If you like a more traditional chili, add another can of beans. If you have time, let the chili rest and then reheat it before serving, as that allows the flavors to develop fully.

Per serving: Calories: 342; Total fat: 3g; Total carbs: 67g; Fiber: 13g; Sugar: 7g; Protein: 13g; Sodium: 537mg

Roasted Curly Beet Salad

SERVES 4
Prep time: 15 minutes
Cook time: 15 minutes

For the vinaigrette

1 garlic clove, finely minced

½ cup olive oil

¼ cup balsamic vinegar

3 tablespoons agave

¼ teaspoon salt

⅛ teaspoon freshly ground black pepper

For the salad

Nonstick cooking spray

4 medium to large beets

6 to 8 cups fresh baby spinach leaves

½ batch Tofu Ricotta (page 173)

½ cup toasted walnuts

½ cup dried cranberries (sweetened or unsweetened)

Salt

Freshly ground black pepper

One of my favorite things about beets, besides how delicious they are, is how many ways you can cook them. Roast them, grill them, pressure-cook them . . . you can even buy them precooked nowadays! Regardless of how I cook them, my favorite way to enjoy beets is in a salad with a nice vinaigrette. I love their earthy, slightly sweet flavor and heartiness.

To make the vinaigrette

In a medium bowl, combine the garlic, olive oil, vinegar, agave, salt, and pepper, and whisk vigorously until thoroughly combined. Transfer to a lidded jar, so you can shake well before serving.

To make the salad

1. Preheat the oven to 350°F. Lightly coat a baking sheet with cooking spray.

2. Spiralize the beets with the Curly Fry blade and trim the spirals to 2- to 3-inch lengths. Transfer the beets to the prepared baking sheet, arrange in a single layer, and bake for 10 to 15 minutes, stirring at least once. Keep an eye on them—spiralized beets roast quickly. Let cool a bit before serving.

3. Divide the spinach onto four plates, and top with the Tofu Ricotta (tablespoon-size dabs), walnuts, cranberries, and beets. Serve the dressing on the side, shaking well before serving and seasoning with salt and pepper to taste.

Per serving: Calories: 508; Total fat: 39g; Total carbs: 35g; Fiber: 6g; Sugar: 25g; Protein: 10g; Sodium: 504mg

Cold Zoodle Salad with Avocado

SERVES 4

Prep time: 15 minutes

½ cup avocado oil

3 tablespoons white balsamic vinegar

1 teaspoon Dijon mustard

¼ teaspoon salt, plus more for seasoning

⅛ teaspoon freshly ground black pepper, plus more for seasoning

1 medium to large zucchini

1 medium summer squash

1 red bell pepper

½ cucumber

1 cup grape tomatoes, quartered

12 fresh basil leaves, torn

2 ripe avocados, halved, pitted, and sliced

Hot summer days call for quick and easy lunches, and you can't get much quicker or easier than this cold salad full of fresh vegetables. The combination of raw veggies (so many colors!) with fresh basil and thick slices of creamy avocado . . . mmmmm! This is exactly the kind of dish you'll find me daydreaming about on a dreary February day. You can use the Angel Hair blade on all the veggies, but I prefer switching up the textures a bit.

1. In a small bowl, whisk together the avocado oil, vinegar, mustard, salt, and pepper. Set aside.

2. Spiralize the zucchini and summer squash using the Angel Hair blade and the red bell pepper and cucumber using the Flat blade. Transfer all the spirals to a large bowl.

3. Add the tomatoes and dressing, and toss to coat.

4. Divide the salad among four bowls, and top with basil and avocado. Season to taste with salt and pepper.

Substitution tip: Cutting back on fat? Substitute your favorite oil-free vinaigrette.

Per serving: Calories: 434; Total fat: 42g; Total carbs: 16g; Fiber: 8g; Sugar: 5g; Protein: 4g; Sodium: 153mg

Sweet 'n' Spicy Fruit Salad

SERVES 4

Prep time: 10 minutes

2 tablespoons freshly squeezed orange juice

2 teaspoons freshly squeezed lime juice

2 teaspoons agave

¼ teaspoon salt

¼ teaspoon chili powder

2 medium pears

1 medium apple

1 mango, peeled and cut into ¼-inch cubes

1 cup fresh strawberries, sliced

1 cup fresh blueberries

This is the perfect side salad to go with a sandwich on a warm summer day, or even a meal all on its own! It's so sweet and citrusy, with just that hint of heat from the chili powder. It's not overpowering, it's more like salt . . . it brings out the natural flavor of the fruit! You can whisk the juice and spices ahead of time, but don't spiralize the pears and apple until you're ready to serve.

1. In a small bowl, whisk together the orange juice, lime juice, agave, salt, and chili powder. Set aside.

2. Spiralize the pears and apple using the Curly Fry blade and trim the spirals to 2- to 3-inch lengths.

3. In a large bowl, combine the pears, apple, mango, strawberries, and blueberries. Add the orange juice mixture and toss to coat.

Serving tip: Serving this fruit salad as part of a boozy brunch? Replace the orange juice with a shot of tequila!

Per serving: Calories: 196; Total fat: 1g; Total carbs: 51g; Fiber: 8g; Sugar: 39g; Protein: 2g; Sodium: 122mg

Autumnal Couscous Salad

SERVES 4 TO 6
Prep time: 10 minutes
Cook time: 15 minutes

For the couscous

1 teaspoon vegan butter

1 cup Israeli couscous

1¼ cups water

½ teaspoon salt

¼ teaspoon freshly ground black pepper

¼ teaspoon garlic powder

For the vinaigrette

2 tablespoons olive oil

2 tablespoons apple cider vinegar

2 tablespoons pure maple syrup

Autumn is my favorite time of year, when cranberries, apples, and butternut squash start making an appearance in all manner of dishes. But since autumn comes just once a year, I created this salad so I could enjoy those flavors all the time. The Israeli (or "pearl") couscous is hearty enough to balance out all the fruits and veggies in this recipe, and the vinaigrette is flavorful and not too sweet. This salad makes a great side, or you can enjoy it as a meal on its own—that's what I do!

To make the couscous

1. In a large saucepan over medium heat, melt the butter.

2. Add the couscous and toast for 3 to 4 minutes, or until golden brown, stirring frequently.

3. Add the water and bring to a boil. Reduce the heat to low, cover the pan, and simmer for 8 to 10 minutes, or until the water is evaporated. Season with salt, pepper, and garlic powder.

To make the vinaigrette

In a small bowl, whisk together the olive oil, vinegar, and maple syrup. Set aside.

CONTINUED

For the salad

1 small butternut squash

2 tablespoons water

1 small jicama (about the size of an apple), rind removed

1 medium to large apple (Honeycrisp or Pink Lady)

2 teaspoons freshly squeezed lemon juice

½ cup chopped walnuts

½ cup dried cranberries (sweetened or unsweetened)

To make the salad

1. Cut off the bulbous end of the butternut squash and reserve for another use. Trim the ends of the remaining neck piece and slice or peel off the rind. Spiralize the neck piece using the Fine Shred blade and trim the spirals to 2- to 3-inch lengths.

2. In a large nonstick skillet over medium heat, heat the water. Add the butternut squash spirals and sauté for 5 to 7 minutes. Remove from the heat.

3. Spiralize the jicama using the Fine Shred blade and trim the spirals to 2- to 3-inch lengths. Add the jicama to the skillet.

4. Spiralize the apple using the Fine Shred blade and trim the spirals to 2- to 3-inch lengths. In a small bowl, toss the apple spirals with the lemon juice to coat. Let sit for 1 to 2 minutes. Drain the excess juice, then add the apple, walnuts, and cranberries to the skillet. Stir well to combine.

Ingredient tip: I prefer sweetened dried cranberries, but if you're cutting back on sugar, use unsweetened.

Per serving: Calories: 533; Total fat: 18g; Total carbs: 87g; Fiber: 16g; Sugar: 23g; Protein: 10g; Sodium: 320mg

Tangy Cucumber Salad

SERVES 4 TO 6

Prep time: 15 minutes

2 medium cucumbers

2½ teaspoons salt, divided

1 red bell pepper

½ sweet onion

⅓ cup sugar

¼ cup rice wine vinegar

A fun take on a traditional picnic side dish! Why eat boring ol' sliced cucumbers when you can eat wavy spiralized ones? However you slice it (*ha!*), cucumbers are good for us. They're high in vitamins C and K, as well as magnesium, potassium, and manganese. They're also a great vessel for hummus, but that's a whole different story.

1. Spiralize the cucumbers using the Coarse Wavy blade and put them in a colander. Toss with 2 teaspoons of salt. Put the colander over a bowl and let sit for 30 minutes. Rinse the cucumbers and squeeze them dry.

2. Spiralize the red bell pepper and onion with the Angel Hair blade and trim the spirals to 1- to 2-inch lengths.

3. In a large bowl, whisk together the sugar, vinegar, and the remaining ½ teaspoon of salt. Add the cucumbers, red bell pepper, and onion. Gently stir to combine, cover the bowl, and refrigerate for 1 hour before serving.

Per serving: Calories: 110; Total fat: 0g; Total carbs: 26g; Fiber: 1g; Sugar: 21g; Protein: 1g; Sodium: 586mg

Mains

Spicy Potato Soft Tacos, page 134

Buffalo Tofu Pizza with Cauliflower Crust

SERVES 4 TO 6
Prep time: 25 minutes
Cook time: 50 minutes

For the crust

2 to 3 tablespoons water

1 medium to large head cauliflower, riced (about 6 cups)

2 vegan eggs (my favorites are Follow Your Heart and Just)

½ cup vegan mozzarella shreds

¼ cup chickpea flour

2 tablespoons cornstarch

1 teaspoon Italian seasoning

½ teaspoon salt

¼ teaspoon garlic powder

⅛ teaspoon freshly ground black pepper

Buffalo sauce is one of those things I didn't know I liked until I went vegan. Wings never appealed to me—even during my "pre-gan" days—so I never really tried the sauce. If you've spent even a few minutes on my blog, you know I'm a huge fan now and put it on nearly anything. Cauliflower, fries, and, of course, tofu! All are good ways to increase your Buffalo sauce intake, but this pizza is hands down the best.

To make the crust

1. Preheat the oven to 400°F.

2. In a large skillet over medium-high heat, heat the water. Add the cauliflower rice and sauté for 4 to 5 minutes, or until heated through. Drain completely. Using a paper towel, gently squeeze out any excess water, then put the rice in a large bowl.

3. Add the eggs, mozzarella shreds, flour, cornstarch, Italian seasoning, salt, garlic powder, and pepper. Mix well.

4. Turn the dough out onto a nonstick pizza pan. Using your hands, press the crust to about a ½-inch thickness, leaving it a little thicker around the edges of the pan. Bake for 20 to 25 minutes, or until firm. Remove and leave the oven on.

For the pizza

Nonstick cooking spray
½ (14-ounce) block firm tofu, drained and pressed for at least 30 minutes, halved horizontally, then each piece halved widthwise (you'll have 4 small rectangles)

¼ cup Buffalo sauce, plus 2 tablespoons

1 small to medium green bell pepper

1 large carrot

¾ cup vegan mozzarella shreds

Ranch Dressing (page 175), for topping

To make the pizza

1. Coat a baking sheet with cooking spray.

2. Arrange the tofu in a single layer on the pan, and bake for 40 minutes, flipping once about halfway through. (You can bake this at the same time as you bake the pizza crust.) When it is finished baking, chop the tofu into bite-size pieces. Put the pieces in a medium bowl, and toss with ¼ cup of Buffalo sauce.

3. Spiralize the green bell pepper and carrot using the Angel Hair blade and trim the spirals to 2- to 3-inch lengths.

4. Spread the remaining 2 tablespoons of Buffalo sauce on the crust. Add the tofu and about half of the green bell pepper and carrot spirals. Top with the mozzarella shreds, and bake the pizza for 10 minutes, or until the crust is golden and crispy and the cheese is melted.

5. Top with the remaining green bell pepper and carrot spirals and serve with the Ranch Dressing.

Per serving: Calories: 260; Total fat: 10g; Total carbs: 35g; Fiber: 9g; Sugar: 8g; Protein: 9g; Sodium: 1261mg

Barbecue Chick'n Pizza with Sweet Potato Crust

SERVES 4 TO 6

Prep time: 20 minutes

Cook time: 25 minutes

For the crust

2 cups mashed
sweet potato

2 cups chickpea flour

¼ cup cornstarch

1 teaspoon salt

For the pizza

¾ cup dry soy curls

1 teaspoon Montreal
chicken seasoning

1 small red onion

1 red bell pepper

1 cup barbecue sauce,
divided

1 cup vegan mozzarella
shreds

¼ to ½ cup chopped fresh
cilantro

I realize cilantro is a controversial topping, so you have my blessing to leave it off . . . but I'm secretly hoping you won't. I love cilantro's fresh, spicy, and almost citrusy bite, which pairs perfectly with barbecue sauce and red onion. I also love the mild sweetness of this pizza crust—it's really just a hint. Please do take the time to create a thick crust around the edges, as it helps hold in the toppings *and* keeps any thin edges from overcooking. Using a vented pizza pan helps any moisture in the crust escape, so it cooks evenly.

To make the crust

1. Preheat the oven to 375°F.

2. In a medium bowl, stir together the sweet potato, flour, cornstarch, and salt, until it forms a ball. Line a pizza pan with parchment paper. Place the dough in the center of the pan, and cover it with a second piece of parchment paper. Use your hands or a rolling pin to smooth and shape the dough. Roll the dough to ½-inch thickness, making a thicker crust around the outside edges of the pan.

3. Remove the top piece of parchment only. Bake the crust for 10 to 15 minutes, or until firm to the touch and crispy.

~~~~~~

To make the pizza

1. Put the soy curls in a bowl of warm water and let sit for 10 minutes. Squeeze out the excess water, and chop the curls, as desired. Put the chopped curls in a medium bowl, add the Montreal seasoning, and toss to mix. Set aside.

2. Spiralize the red onion and red bell pepper using the Angel Hair blade and trim the spirals to 2- to 3-inch lengths.

3. Using a spatula, loosen the crust from the parchment (but don't remove the paper). Very little, if any, dough should stick to it. Spread ⅔ cup of barbecue sauce over the crust, leaving the slightly thicker edge uncovered.

4. Top with the soy curls, veggie spirals, moz-zarella shreds, and the remaining ⅓ cup of barbecue sauce.

5. Bake the pizza for 5 to 10 minutes, or until the crust is crispy and the cheese is melted.

6. Sprinkle with cilantro, and serve.

Substitution tip: No soy curls? Any mock chick'n will work—just be sure to chop it into bite-size pieces.

Per serving: Calories: 534; Total fat: 16g; Total carbs: 82g; Fiber: 8g; Sugar: 26g; Protein: 15g; Sodium: 1602mg

Roasted Beet Pizza

SERVES 4 TO 6
Prep time: 25 minutes
Cook time: 20 minutes

For the dough

½ cup lukewarm water

1 teaspoon active dry yeast

1¼ cups unbleached all-purpose flour, plus more for the work surface

1 large red beet, roasted and puréed smooth

3 teaspoons agave

½ teaspoon salt, plus more as needed

1 teaspoon olive oil

For the pizza

Nonstick cooking spray

3 golden beets

½ teaspoon salt, plus more as needed

⅛ teaspoon freshly ground black pepper, plus more as needed

½ batch Tofu Ricotta (page 173)

8 to 10 fresh basil leaves, torn

When I first went vegan in 2010, ordering a pizza wasn't an option, and making my own was daunting (this was right around the time I was learning to cook). These days, there are a handful of pizzerias that will deliver a 100 percent plant-based pie to my door. But you know what? I'd rather make my own! Sometimes I go with the traditional tomato sauce and mozzarella combination, but I also like to play around with new ideas, like ricotta and roasted golden beets . . . and red beets in the crust.

To make the dough

1. In a large bowl, stir together the water and yeast until the yeast is completely dissolved. Let sit for 5 minutes.

2. Add the flour, beet purée, agave, and salt. Using your hands, mix the dough just until it comes together.

3. Turn the dough out onto a clean work surface dusted with flour. Knead the dough for 4 to 5 minutes, until all the flour is absorbed and the dough is stretchy but smooth. If dough sticks to your fingers, add a small amount of flour to the dough. Roll the dough into a ball.

4. Coat a large bowl with the olive oil. Place the dough in the bowl, and turn it to completely coat with the oil. Cover the bowl and place in a warm area to rise for at least 90 minutes.

1. Preheat the oven to 350°F. Coat a baking sheet with cooking spray.

2. Spiralize the beets using the Curly Fry blade. Arrange the beet spirals in a single layer on the baking sheet, and season with salt and pepper. Roast for 10 minutes, stirring once about halfway through.

3. Increase the oven temperature to 475°F.

4. When the dough has doubled in size, roll or stretch it into a 12-inch circle. Place the dough on a nonstick pizza pan and bake for 5 minutes. Remove from the oven.

5. Schmear the Tofu Ricotta evenly over the center of the dough to about ½-inch from the edges. Top with the beet spirals.

6. Bake the pizza for 4 to 5 minutes, or until the ricotta is warmed through and the pizza crust is firm to the touch and crispy.

7. Top with the basil, and season to taste with salt and pepper.

Substitution tip: Cutting back on carbs? Swap out this dough for one made with cauliflower (see Buffalo Tofu Pizza with Cauliflower Crust, page 106) or sweet potato (see Barbecue Chick'n Pizza with Sweet Potato Crust, page 108).

Per serving: Calories: 325; Total fat: 6g; Total carbs: 59g; Fiber: 1g; Sugar: 5g; Protein: 24g; Sodium: 847mg

Sweet Corn Butternut Squash Flatbread

SERVES 4

Prep time: 10 minutes

Cook time: 8 minutes

1 medium butternut squash

2 to 3 tablespoons water

1 teaspoon freshly squeezed lime juice

¼ teaspoon chili powder

4 (6-inch) pieces naan, lightly toasted

2 ripe avocados, halved, pitted, and lightly mashed

2 ears fresh corn, cooked and kernels cut from the cobs

8 fresh basil leaves, torn

½ teaspoon salt

¼ teaspoon freshly ground black pepper

This delicious flatbread just screams summer to me. It's light yet filling, and also beautiful—especially if you grill the corn and it has char marks on it! You may be tempted to skip the chili powder on the butternut squash, but don't. It adds a nice balance to the sweet corn and the cool, creamy avocado. Is there anything better than this combination on a summer day?

1. Cut off the bulbous end of the butternut squash and reserve for another use. Trim the end of the remaining neck piece and slice or peel off the rind. Spiralize the neck using the Angel Hair blade and trim the spirals to 2- to 3-inch lengths.

2. In a large skillet over medium-high heat, heat the water. Add the butternut squash spirals and sauté for 5 to 7 minutes. Drain any excess water and stir in the lime juice and chili powder.

3. Place the naan pieces on a clean work surface, and schmear each evenly with avocado. Stir the squash and corn together, and top the naan with the veggie mixture. Finally, add the basil, salt, and pepper. These can be eaten with your hands, or with a knife and fork!

Per serving: Calories: 434; Total fat: 20g; Total carbs: 60g; Fiber: 13g; Sugar: 6g; Protein: 10g; Sodium: 260mg

Garlicky Lemon Broccoli Noodles

SERVES 4

Prep time: 10 minutes
Cook time: 19 minutes

1 (10-inch) broccoli stalk

1 medium sweet potato

2 tablespoons avocado oil

4 cups broccoli florets

½ teaspoon salt

⅛ teaspoon freshly ground black pepper

1 batch Garlicky Lemon Cream Sauce (page 174)

Nutritional yeast, for topping

When I was a kid, broccoli was probably the most commonly served vegetable side. Of course, it was covered in melted cheese, but still, it was broccoli! Like most people, we really only ate the florets and threw away the stalks—and that's one of my favorite things about this dish: We can finally use those stalks!

1. Spiralize the broccoli stalk and sweet potato using the Angel Hair blade and trim the spirals to 4- to 5-inch lengths.

2. In a large skillet over medium-high heat, heat the avocado oil until it shimmers.

3. Add the broccoli and sweet potato spirals, broccoli florets, and salt and pepper. Cook for 8 to 10 minutes, or until the spirals are soft (the florets will need more time).

4. Add the Garlicky Lemon Cream Sauce and bring the mixture to a simmer. Reduce the heat to low and simmer, uncovered, for 6 to 8 minutes, or until the florets are tender.

5. Sprinkle with nutritional yeast, and serve.

Per serving: Calories: 199; Total fat: 10g; Total carbs: 24g; Fiber: 8g; Sugar: 4g; Protein: 6g; Sodium: 711mg

Creamy Buffalo Zoodles

SERVES 4

Prep time: 10 minutes

Cook time: 8 minutes

8 medium to large zucchini

2 to 3 tablespoons water

8 ounces vegan cream cheese

½ cup Buffalo sauce

Spiralizing is an easy and fun way to lighten some of your favorite dishes, and this recipe is a perfect example. I used to enjoy this creamy Buffalo sauce on a big ol' bowl of pasta, which was delicious but left me feeling weighed down. Instead, combining it with zucchini zoodles offers all the same flavor but with more nutrients and far fewer carbs and calories.

1. Spiralize the zucchini using the Curly Fry blade.

2. In a large skillet over medium-high heat, heat the water. Add the zoodles and cook for 3 to 4 minutes. Remove from the heat and drain the excess water.

3. In a small saucepan over medium heat, combine the cream cheese and Buffalo sauce, stirring until blended.

4. Return the skillet with the zoodles to low heat. Pour the cream sauce over them. Stir to coat and cook for 2 to 3 minutes, until warmed through. Serve hot.

Per serving: Calories: 243; Total fat: 17g; Total carbs: 19g; Fiber: 8g; Sugar: 9g; Protein: 9g; Sodium: 318mg

Red Lentil Curry

SERVES 4

Prep time: 10 minutes
Cook time: 22 minutes

2 medium sweet potatoes

3 large carrots

1 small sweet onion

1 to 2 tablespoons vegetable oil

1 garlic clove, minced

1½ tablespoons Thai red curry paste

1 teaspoon garam masala

½ teaspoon sugar

¼ teaspoon ground turmeric

¼ teaspoon ground ginger

½ cup finely diced tomatoes, with their juices, plus more for topping (optional)

¼ cup coconut milk

1 cup dry red lentils, cooked according to the package instructions

Sliced avocado, for topping (optional)

Chopped fresh cilantro, for topping (optional)

This curry is so good, you may want to keep all four servings for yourself. Curry is usually served over rice, but this one has lots of veggie noodles—so go ahead and have some extra; it's okay. If you're new to cooking lentils, you can usually find them with the dry rice in your grocery store.

1. Spiralize the sweet potatoes, carrots, and onion using the Angel Hair blade and trim the spirals to 2- to 3-inch lengths.

2. In a large skillet over medium-high heat, heat the vegetable oil until it shimmers.

3. Add the onion and garlic. Sauté for 2 to 3 minutes.

4. Add the sweet potato and carrot spirals, curry paste, garam masala, sugar, turmeric, and ginger. Stir well to coat. Cook for 4 to 5 minutes more.

5. Stir in the tomatoes and their juices, coconut milk, and lentils. Reduce the heat to low, and simmer for 10 to 15 minutes, or until the lentils are tender.

6. Serve topped with tomato, avocado, and cilantro, as desired.

Ingredient tip: Garam masala is a spice blend used in many Indian dishes. You can find it in most grocery stores with spices or in the international food aisle.

Per serving: Calories: 435; Total fat: 16g; Total carbs: 56g; Fiber: 19g; Sugar: 9g; Protein: 15g; Sodium: 1010mg

Tofu Sweet Potato Pad Thai

SERVES 4
Prep time: 15 minutes
Cook time: 25 minutes

For the sauce

¼ cup vegetable broth

3 tablespoons light brown sugar

2 tablespoons vegetarian fish sauce

2 tablespoons soy sauce

1 tablespoon freshly squeezed lime juice

1½ teaspoons *sambal oelek*

When I traveled through Southeast Asia, fish sauce was in *everything*, even dishes considered vegetarian, so that was a challenge. Thankfully, I was still able to eat plenty of noodles free of fish sauce, because I love noodles! But sometimes I want more veggies and fewer noodles, and that's why this recipe exists. I've replaced the traditional rice noodles with sweet potato noodles. If you want to make your pad Thai a bit more filling, you can also go half 'n' half. As for the fish sauce, there are vegetarian versions available online and in stores.

To make the sauce

In a small saucepan over medium heat, whisk together the vegetable broth, brown sugar, fish sauce, soy sauce, lime juice, and *sambal oelek*. Bring to a simmer and cook for 1 minute. Remove from the heat and set aside.

To make the pad Thai

1. Spiralize the sweet potatoes using the Angel Hair blade.

2. In a large skillet over medium-high heat, heat 1 tablespoon of sesame oil until it shimmers.

3. Add the sweet potato spirals and sauté for 8 to 10 minutes, or until soft. Remove them from the skillet and set aside.

4. Return the skillet to the heat and add the remaining 1 tablespoon of sesame oil, heating until it shimmers.

For the pad Thai

2 medium to large sweet potatoes

2 tablespoons sesame oil, divided

1 (14-ounce) block firm tofu, drained, pressed for at least 1 hour, and cubed

2 garlic cloves, minced

2 medium carrots, thinly sliced

1 red bell pepper, thinly sliced

½ sweet onion, thinly sliced

4 scallions (green parts only), thinly sliced

⅓ cup chopped roasted peanuts

Fresh basil, for topping (optional)

Bean sprouts, for topping (optional)

Lime wedges, for topping (optional)

5. Add the tofu and sauté for 2 to 3 minutes, turning as needed so the cubes brown evenly.

6. Add the garlic. Cook and turn the tofu for 2 to 3 minutes more.

7. Add the carrots, red bell pepper, onion, and sauce. Cook for 4 to 5 minutes, or until the veggies start to soften.

8. Stir in the sweet potato spirals, cover the skillet, and remove it from the heat. Let sit for a few minutes before serving. Top with scallions and peanuts. Garnish with basil, bean sprouts, and lime wedges as desired.

Ingredient tip: *Sambal oelek* is a garlicky chili sauce that has become very easy to find—I've even seen it on restaurant tables alongside ketchup! If you don't have it on hand, any Asian hot sauce will work.

Per serving: Calories: 237; Total fat: 17g; Total carbs: 33g; Fiber: 6g; Sugar: 15g; Protein: 15g; Sodium: 1319mg

Ruby Ribbon Alfredo

SERVES 4

Prep time: 15 minutes

Cook time: 17 minutes

1 medium butternut squash

2 medium to large sweet potatoes

3 medium beets

2 to 3 tablespoons water

1 batch Alfredo Sauce (page 172)

Salt

Freshly ground black pepper

Fresh herbs of choice, for topping

In case you're wondering about the name of this dish, it's because beets are nature's food coloring, and they make this creamy dish the loveliest shade of red! Well, until you add the Alfredo—then it's pink . . . which happens to be my favorite color, so I'm okay with that. If you want to make it more of a rainbow, skip the beets and add your favorite vegetables. Zucchini and bell peppers work well!

1. Cut off the bulbous end of the butternut squash and reserve for another use. Trim the ends of the remaining neck piece and slice or peel off the rind. Spiralize the squash, sweet potatoes, and beets using the Coarse Shred blade and trim the spirals to 4- to 5-inch lengths.

2. In a large nonstick skillet over medium-high heat, heat the water. Add the veggie spirals and sauté for 8 to 10 minutes, or until soft. Remove from the heat, and drain any remaining liquid from the skillet. Use paper towels to gently squeeze any excess water from the spirals, then return the spirals to the hot skillet and place over low heat.

3. Stir in the Alfredo Sauce. Cover the skillet and cook for 4 to 5 minutes, or until the sauce and veggies are heated through. Season to taste with salt and pepper. Serve topped with your favorite fresh herbs.

Per serving: Calories: 233; Total fat: 4g; Total carbs: 41g; Fiber: 7g; Sugar: 13g; Protein: 13g; Sodium: 354mg

Tex-Mex Potato Noodle Pie

SERVES 4 TO 6

Prep time: 20 minutes
Cook time: 55 minutes

Nonstick cooking spray

4 large Yukon gold
potatoes

2 tablespoons vegetable
oil, divided

¼ teaspoon salt

⅛ teaspoon freshly
ground black pepper

1 vegan egg (my favorites
are Follow Your Heart and
Just)

1 small sweet onion, diced

1 garlic clove, minced

½ teaspoon smoked
paprika

½ teaspoon ground cumin

½ teaspoon red pepper
flakes

You may be wondering what the heck a potato noodle pie is, so let me explain. It's like spaghetti pie (of which I am a ginormous fan) but with potato noodles instead of spaghetti. And it's spicy, hence the Tex-Mex name!

1. Preheat the oven to 350°F. Lightly coat a 9-inch pie pan with cooking spray.

2. Spiralize the potatoes using the Angel Hair blade and trim the spirals to 3- to 4-inch lengths. Quickly rinse the spirals with water.

3. In a large skillet over medium-high heat, heat 1 tablespoon of vegetable oil until it shimmers.

4. Add the potato spirals, salt, and pepper. Sauté for 8 to 10 minutes, or until the spirals are just barely soft. Transfer them to a large bowl and add the egg. Use your hands to mix the spirals and egg completely, then press the mixture into the pie pan in a thin layer covering the bottom and sides of the pan, as though you were forming a piecrust. Bake, uncovered, for 15 to 20 minutes, or until the potato "crust" is firm to the touch.

5. Return the skillet to medium-high heat, and heat the remaining 1 tablespoon of vegetable oil until it shimmers.

6. Add the onion, garlic, paprika, cumin, and red pepper flakes. Cook for 2 to 3 minutes, or until fragrant.

CONTINUED

1 red bell pepper, cut into ¼-inch pieces

4 cups fresh baby spinach leaves

2 spicy vegan sausages, halved and sliced

½ batch Tofu Ricotta (page 173)

¾ to 1 cup spaghetti sauce (depending on how saucy you want it)

½ cup vegan mozzarella shreds

7. Add the red bell pepper and cook for 2 minutes more. Stir in the spinach and sausage, cover the skillet, and remove it from the heat. Let sit for a few minutes.

8. Stir in the Tofu Ricotta. Transfer the mixture to the piecrust and spread evenly. Top with the spaghetti sauce and mozzarella shreds. Cover the pie pan with foil and bake for 15 minutes.

9. Remove the foil and bake for 5 more minutes, or until the cheese melts. Cut and serve.

Ingredient tip: The Field Roast brand has a chipotle sausage that is delicious and very, very spicy—that's what I use in this recipe.

Per serving: Calories: 507; Total fat: 15g; Total carbs: 78g; Fiber: 15g; Sugar: 11g; Protein: 18g; Sodium: 1047mg

Sausage and Zucchini Noodle Lasagna Casserole

SERVES 4 TO 6
Prep time: 20 minutes
Cook time: 35 minutes

3 medium zucchini

1 tablespoon water

2 red bell peppers, thinly sliced

1 small sweet onion, thinly sliced

¼ teaspoon salt

⅛ teaspoon freshly ground black pepper

3 cups spaghetti sauce, divided

1 batch Tofu Ricotta (page 173)

2 vegan Italian sausages, sliced

1½ cups vegan mozzarella shreds

Fresh basil leaves, for topping

This casserole is a veggie-fied version of my go-to lasagna, which itself is a take on sausage-and-pepper sub sandwiches. Which is to say, it's gotten healthier and healthier with each ingredient change! it's important to squeeze as much liquid as you can out of the zucchini after you sauté it. This casserole also has very little sauce in it during baking (to avoid a soggy situation). But it's all good, because you can heat up the extra sauce and serve it on the side. Use a gravy boat and make it fun!

1. Preheat the oven to 400°F.

2. Spiralize the zucchini using the Flat blade.

3. In a large skillet over medium-high heat, heat the water. Add the zucchini spirals, red bell pepper, and onion. Cook for 3 to 4 minutes. Drain any remaining water, and use paper towels to gently squeeze out any excess liquid. Sprinkle the vegetables with salt and pepper, and set aside.

4. Spread 2 tablespoons of spaghetti sauce on the bottom of a 2½-quart baking dish. Add about half the cooked vegetables. Spread half of the Tofu Ricotta over the vegetables, and top with 1 cup of spaghetti sauce, spreading evenly. (The ricotta is thick and may be difficult to spread, but the sauce will help!) Using the back of a spoon, press everything down into the baking dish.

CONTINUED

5. Scatter half the sausage slices and ½ cup of mozzarella shreds on top of the sauce. Top with the remaining cooked vegetables, the remaining Tofu Ricotta, 1 cup of sauce, the remaining sausage slices, and the remaining mozzarella shreds. Press everything down again. Cover the baking dish with foil and bake for 30 minutes.

6. Remove the foil and let the casserole rest for 10 minutes before serving. Top with fresh basil and serve the remaining sauce, heated, on the side.

Serving tip: Use a slotted spoon to serve, as some zucchini juice may have accumulated at the bottom of the baking dish.

Substitution tip: Avoiding processed foods? Skip the sausage and add more veggies!

Per serving: Calories: 387; Total fat: 18g; Total carbs: 41g; Fiber: 9g; Sugar: 16g; Protein: 20g; Sodium: 1896mg

Super Squash Lasagna with White Sauce

SERVES 4 TO 6

Prep time: 20 minutes

Cook time: 40 minutes

1 small butternut squash

1 small summer squash

1 small zucchini

Salt

Freshly ground black pepper

1 batch Alfredo Sauce (page 172)

6 oven-ready lasagna noodles

1 batch Tofu Ricotta (page 173)

½ cup vegan mozzarella shreds

I love lasagna. YOU love lasagna. We all love lasagna. This version is fun because it uses a white sauce (which is both decadent and delicious) and also provides a whole mess of vitamins and nutrients. With three different squashes in this recipe, you're getting vitamins A, B_6, C, and E, as well as folate, magnesium, and fiber. I've included my recipes for Alfredo Sauce (page 172) and Tofu Ricotta (page 173), but (thankfully!) there are premade vegan versions available in stores and online.

1. Preheat the oven to 400°F.

2. Cut off the bulbous end of the butternut squash and reserve for another use. Trim the ends of the remaining neck piece and slice or peel off the rind. Spiralize the butternut squash, summer squash, and zucchini using the Angel Hair blade. Toss the spirals together and season with salt and pepper.

3. Spread the bottom of a 7-by-11-inch baking dish with 2 to 3 tablespoons of Alfredo Sauce in a thin layer. Place three lasagna noodles (breaking them, as needed, for complete coverage) on top of the sauce.

4. Add half the Tofu Ricotta, spreading it evenly over the noodles, followed by ½ cup of Alfredo Sauce. Top with half the squash spirals and three more lasagna noodles. Press down on the noodles to compress the ingredients.

CONTINUED

5. Finish layering with the remaining ricotta, another ½ cup of Alfredo Sauce, and the rest of the squash. Sprinkle the mozzarella shreds evenly over the top, and drizzle with the remaining Alfredo Sauce. Season to taste with salt and pepper.

6. Cover the dish with foil and bake for 40 minutes.

7. Remove the foil for the last 10 minutes of cooking. The lasagna is done when it's bubbly and the cheese is melted.

Preparation tip: Want it cheesier? Double the mozzarella and add another layer with the Alfredo Sauce in step 4.

Per serving: Calories: 433; Total fat: 16g; Total carbs: 54; Fiber: 8g; Sugar: 9g; Protein: 26g; Sodium: 596mg

Chickpea "Tuna" Casserole

SERVES 4 TO 6

Prep time: 15 minutes
Cook time: 40 minutes

Nonstick cooking spray

1 (15.5-ounce) can chickpeas, 1 tablespoon liquid reserved, then rinsed and drained

1 teaspoon Old Bay seasoning

⅛ teaspoon freshly ground black pepper

5 medium to large Yukon gold potatoes

1 garlic clove, minced

½ sweet onion, diced

2 cups fresh baby spinach leaves

1 red bell pepper, diced

1 cup sliced baby bella mushrooms

1 cup vegan cheddar shreds

½ cup cashew milk

½ cup panko bread crumbs

This is absolutely not your mom's tuna casserole! There's no cream soup from a can, no pasta, and no peas in sight. Instead, it's a lighter take on the classic many of us ate as children (or as adults—this is a judgment-free zone!), and one you can feel good about eating. There's still a bit of "cheese" in there (*because, casserole*), but without the roux and with potatoes replacing the pasta, this is a healthy, feel-good, and comforting dish!

1. Preheat the oven to 400°F. Lightly coat a 2½-quart casserole dish with cooking spray.

2. In a food processor, combine the chickpeas, reserved liquid, Old Bay, and pepper. Give the chickpeas five to six quick pulses, and set aside.

3. Spiralize the potatoes using the Curly Fry blade and trim the spirals to 3- to 4-inch lengths.

4. In a large nonstick skillet over medium-high heat, heat about ¼ cup of water. Add the garlic and onion and sauté for 2 to 3 minutes.

5. Add the potato spirals and cook for 5 to 7 minutes.

6. Add the spinach, red bell pepper, and mushrooms. Cook for 2 to 3 minutes, stirring occasionally. Remove the skillet from the heat.

CONTINUED

7. Stir in the chickpea mixture, cheddar, and milk, mixing well. Transfer the mixture to the casserole dish, and top with the bread crumbs. Spritz the top of the casserole with a bit of cooking spray, cover the dish with foil, and bake for 25 minutes.

8. Remove the foil during the last 10 minutes of cooking time to brown the top. Cool before serving.

Ingredient tip: Chickpeas, also known as garbanzo beans, are low in calories yet high in fiber and protein. They also have a mild taste and work well in lots of recipes.

Per serving: Calories: 462; Total fat: 9g; Total carbs: 84g; Fiber: 13g; Sugar: 6g; Protein: 13g; Sodium: 728mg

Cheesy Cauliflower and Broccoli Casserole

SERVES 4 TO 6
Prep time: 10 minutes
Cook time: 30 minutes

Nonstick cooking spray

½ cup dry soy curls

½ teaspoon Montreal chicken seasoning

1 large head cauliflower, cut into florets (3 cups)

1 (6-inch) broccoli stalk

2 tablespoons vegetable oil

4 cups broccoli florets

¼ teaspoon garlic powder

¼ teaspoon salt

⅛ teaspoon freshly ground black pepper

1½ tablespoons vegan butter

1½ tablespoons all-purpose flour

1½ cups unsweetened cashew milk

1½ cups vegan cheddar shreds

½ cup panko bread crumbs

This casserole is everything. It's rich, creamy, and cheesy with just enough salt (okay, I actually add extra to mine). And there are crunchy panko crumbs on top! It's basically mac 'n' cheese but with cruciferous vegetables instead of pasta—and it's just as good! Plus, it has broccoli noodles, which are an amazing way to use the broccoli stalks that most people throw out. The stalks might be your new favorite part of broccoli!

1. Preheat the oven to 350°F. Coat a 7-by-11-inch baking dish with cooking spray.

2. In a medium bowl, combine the soy curls with enough warm water to cover them, and let sit for 10 minutes. When soft, drain and squeeze out the excess liquid. Chop the curls into bite-size pieces, and transfer them to another medium bowl. Add the Montreal seasoning and toss to coat. Set aside.

3. Rice the cauliflower using the Flat blade. Spiralize the broccoli stem using the Angel Hair blade.

4. In a large skillet over medium-high heat, heat the vegetable oil until it shimmers.

5. Add the cauliflower rice and the broccoli spirals and florets. Stir in the garlic powder, salt, and pepper, and cook for 3 to 5 minutes, stirring occasionally. Remove from the skillet and set aside.

CONTINUED

6. Return the skillet (no need to rinse) to medium-high heat, and melt the butter completely. Stir in the flour and cook for 2 to 3 minutes. Whisk in the milk until smooth. Simmer the mixture for about 2 minutes, until it begins to thicken. Whisk in the cheddar shreds and turn off the heat.

7. Add the soy curls and cooked vegetables to the skillet, and stir until they're completely coated with the sauce. Pour the entire mixture into the prepared baking dish and top with the bread crumbs. Spritz the top of the casserole with a little cooking spray and bake, uncovered, for 20 minutes.

Per serving: Calories: 420; Total fat: 23g; Total carbs: 44g; Fiber: 11g; Sugar: 8g; Protein: 13g; Sodium: 795mg

Korean-Style Barbecue Meatballs with Potato Noodles

SERVES 4

Prep time: 15 minutes

Cook time: 40 minutes

For the sauce

3 tablespoons lite soy sauce

3 tablespoons light brown sugar

2 tablespoons water

1 to 2 tablespoons gochujang sauce

1 tablespoon sesame oil

1 tablespoon rice wine vinegar

1 teaspoon minced garlic

½ teaspoon onion powder

My friend Shawna, who is Korean-American, introduced me to Korean recipes back in 2012. I've been obsessed ever since! Of all the flavors used in traditional dishes, Korean barbecue sauce is my 100 percent favorite. It's spicy, with just a hint of sweetness, and is good on pretty much everything. Seriously. If you want to save time, most grocery stores carry premade versions that, though not as good as mine, are pretty yummy.

To make the sauce

In a medium bowl, whisk together the soy sauce, brown sugar, water, gochujang sauce, sesame oil, vinegar, garlic, and onion powder. Set aside.

To make the potato noodles and meatballs

1. Spiralize the Yukon gold and sweet potatoes using the Angel Hair blade.

2. In a large nonstick skillet over medium-high heat, heat 2 to 3 tablespoons of water. Add the potato spirals, garlic powder, onion powder, and salt. Sauté for 8 to 10 minutes, or until soft, adding more water as needed, but you want to end with a dry pan. Transfer the potatoes to a large bowl.

CONTINUED

For the potato noodles and meatballs

3 medium to large Yukon gold potatoes

1 large sweet potato

¼ cup water, plus 2 to 3 tablespoons

½ teaspoon garlic powder

½ teaspoon onion powder

¼ teaspoon salt

12 frozen vegan meatballs

Sesame seeds, for topping (optional)

Sliced scallions (green parts only), for topping (optional)

Hot sauce, for topping (optional)

3. Return the skillet to the heat. Pour the sauce and ¼ cup of water into the pan and stir. Bring the sauce to a simmer and add the meatballs. Reduce the heat to maintain a simmer, cover the skillet, and cook for 5 minutes, stirring occasionally.

4. Remove the cover and simmer for about 20 minutes more. The dish is done when the meatballs are hot all the way through and the sauce has reduced to 1 or 2 thick tablespoons.

5. Remove the skillet from the heat, stir in the cooked vegetables, and re-cover the skillet. Let sit for 2 to 3 minutes while the potato spirals absorb the remaining sauce. Serve topped with the sesame seeds, scallions, and hot sauce, as desired.

Ingredient tip: Gochujang is a hot sauce often used in Korean cooking. It's very thick and is made from chile peppers, sticky rice, soybeans, and salt. You can find it in most grocery stores in the international food aisle.

Per serving: Calories: 440; Total fat: 15g; Total carbs: 55g; Fiber: 11g; Sugar: 15g; Protein: 24g; Sodium: 1512mg

Japchae

SERVES 4
Prep time: 15 minutes,
plus 30 to 60 minutes
marinating time
Cook time: 55 minutes

For the tofu

⅓ cup lite soy sauce

3 tablespoons light brown sugar

2 tablespoons rice wine vinegar

½ teaspoon garlic powder

1 (14-ounce) block firm tofu, drained, pressed for at least 30 minutes, halved horizontally, then each piece halved widthwise (you'll have 4 small rectangles)

Nonstick cooking spray

Japchae is a sweet and savory Korean stir-fry traditionally made with *dangmyeon* ("cellophane" noodles made from sweet potato starch), meat, and vegetables. Obviously, we're cutting out the meat, but we're also replacing the *dangmyeon* with spiralized sweet potatoes. Why eat noodles made with just the starch when you can have the whole *dang* sweet potato?! (Dad joke for the win!)

To make the tofu

1. In a large shallow bowl, whisk together the soy sauce, brown sugar, vinegar, and garlic powder.

2. Add the tofu and marinate for 30 to 60 minutes, flipping at least once.

3. Preheat the oven to 375°F. Coat a baking sheet with cooking spray.

4. Place the tofu rectangles (reserving the remaining marinade) on the prepared baking sheet and bake for 30 to 35 minutes, flipping once about halfway through. The tofu is done when it's lightly browned and starting to crisp.

5. Slice the tofu into thin strips and set aside.

CONTINUED

For the *japchae*

2 medium sweet potatoes

¼ cup water, plus 2 to 3 tablespoons

1 tablespoon vegetable oil, plus more as needed

1 garlic clove, minced

1 small onion, thinly sliced

1 bell pepper, any color, thinly sliced

1 cup sliced white button mushrooms

2 cups fresh baby spinach leaves, cut into long, thin strips

1 large carrot, shredded

½ small cucumber, thinly sliced lengthwise

1 scallion (green part only), thinly sliced, for topping

Toasted sesame seeds, for topping

To make the *japchae*

1. Spiralize the sweet potatoes using the Angel Hair blade and trim the spirals to 4- to 5-inch lengths.

2. In a large nonstick skillet over medium-high heat, heat the water. Add the sweet potato spirals, and sauté for 8 to 10 minutes, or until soft. Remove the spirals and set aside. Pour out any remaining water from the skillet.

3. Return the skillet to medium-high heat, and heat the vegetable oil until it shimmers.

4. Add the garlic and onion and sauté for 2 to 3 minutes.

5. Add the bell pepper and mushrooms, and cook for 2 to 3 minutes more, adding more oil to the skillet, as needed.

6. Stir in the spinach, carrot, cucumber, sweet potato noodles, tofu strips, reserved marinade, and ¼ cup of water. Cover the skillet and reduce the heat to low. Cook for 2 to 3 minutes. Stir well, and serve topped with scallion and sesame seeds.

Per serving: Calories: 233; Total fat: 8g; Total carbs: 32g; Fiber: 5g; Sugar: 16g; Protein: 13g; Sodium: 1251mg

Ratatouille

SERVES 4

Prep time: 10 minutes
Cook time: 23 minutes

2 bell peppers, any color

2 medium to large zucchini

1 small sweet onion

1 medium to large summer squash

2 to 3 tablespoons water

2 garlic cloves, minced

1 cup sliced baby bella mushrooms

1 (28-ounce) can diced tomatoes (with their juices)

1 teaspoon dried oregano

½ teaspoon salt, plus more as needed

¼ teaspoon freshly ground black pepper, plus more as needed

12 fresh basil leaves, thinly sliced, for topping

Ratatouille is a summer vegetable stew that hails from 18th-century France and offers an excellent way to use up all that produce in your refrigerator you're just not sure what to do with. It's usually made with quite a bit of olive oil, but I lightened this version by water-sautéing the veggies. What to do with all those saved calories? My vote is for crusty garlic bread smothered in vegan butter!

1. Spiralize the bell peppers, zucchini, onion, and squash using the Angel Hair blade.

2. In a large nonstick skillet over medium-high heat, heat the water. Add the garlic and onion, and sauté for 2 to 3 minutes. Add the bell peppers, zucchini, and squash, and sauté for 5 minutes more.

3. Stir in the mushrooms, tomatoes and their juices, oregano, salt, and pepper, and bring the mixture to a boil. Reduce the heat to low and simmer for 10 to 15 minutes, just until the veggies are soft. Season to taste with more salt and pepper. Garnish with the basil and serve.

Per serving: Calories: 95; Total fat: 1g; Total carbs: 21g; Fiber: 6g; Sugar: 12g; Protein: 5g; Sodium: 319mg

Spicy Potato Soft Tacos

Lots of fast-food restaurants are jumping on the plant-based bandwagon these days (*And who can blame them? Veganism is the future!*), but when I first went vegan back in 2010, there really weren't many options for me. Fast-food tacos had always been a guilty pleasure, which was why I originally created a potato soft taco recipe on my blog. This is my updated, spiralized, spicier version, and I love it more than ever! If you like more heat, I recommend topping these tacos with your favorite hot sauce for that extra kick.

SERVES 4

Prep time: 15 minutes, plus overnight to soak
Cook time: 25 minutes

For the spicy sauce

⅔ cup cashews, soaked in water overnight and drained

½ cup unsweetened cashew milk

2 to 4 chipotle peppers in adobo sauce, plus 2 tablespoons of the sauce

Juice of 1 lime

1 teaspoon ground cumin

½ teaspoon smoked paprika

½ teaspoon salt

To make the spicy sauce

In a blender, combine the cashews, cashew milk, chipotles, adobo sauce, lime juice, cumin, paprika, and salt. Blend until smooth and set aside.

To make the tacos

1. Preheat the oven to 400°F. Lightly coat a baking sheet with cooking spray.

2. Spiralize the potatoes using the Curly Fry blade and trim the spirals to 2- to 3-inch lengths. Using paper towels, squeeze the spirals dry and put them in a medium bowl. Add the olive oil, rosemary, salt, and pepper, and toss to coat. Arrange the potato spirals on the prepared baking sheet in a single layer.

3. Bake the potato spirals for 20 to 25 minutes, or until they start to brown, stirring at least twice during the baking time.

For the tacos

Nonstick cooking spray

3 medium Yukon gold potatoes

2 tablespoons olive oil

½ teaspoon dried rosemary

¼ teaspoon salt

⅛ teaspoon freshly ground black pepper

8 tortillas

1 cup shredded romaine lettuce

Zest of 1 lime

Chopped fresh cilantro, for topping (optional)

Hot sauce, for topping (optional)

Vegan cheese shreds of choice, for topping (optional)

4. Assemble the tacos, starting with the roasted potato noodles, then a drizzle (or two!) of the spicy sauce, a sprinkle of lettuce and lime zest, and any additional toppings, as desired.

Per serving: Calories: 389; Total fat: 16g; Total carbs: 57g; Fiber: 10g; Sugar: 6g; Protein: 9g; Sodium: 969mg

Chick'n Fajitas

SERVES 4 TO 6
Prep time: 10 minutes
Cook time: 10 minutes

1½ cups dry soy curls

1 small sweet onion

1 red bell pepper

1 small zucchini

4 tablespoons water, divided

½ teaspoon smoked paprika

3 teaspoons fajita seasoning

Salt

Freshly ground black pepper

8 to 12 soft taco flour tortillas

1 cup guacamole

1 jalapeño pepper, thinly sliced

Vegan sour cream, for topping (optional)

Vegan cheese shreds of choice, for topping (optional)

Salsa, for topping (optional)

Chopped fresh cilantro, for topping (optional)

What makes these fajitas different from others? Smoked paprika and beautiful spiral vegetables! If you don't have soy curls on hand, use any mock chick'n, chopped into small pieces.

1. In a large bowl, combine the soy curls with enough warm water to cover them. Let soak for at least 10 minutes. Drain and squeeze them completely dry. Chop any larger curls into bite-size pieces.

2. Spiralize the onion, red bell pepper, and zucchini using the Fine Shred blade and trim the spirals to 2- to 3-inch lengths.

3. In a large skillet over medium heat, heat 2 to 3 tablespoons of water. Add the onion and red bell pepper spirals, and sauté for 2 minutes.

4. Add the zucchini spirals and cook for 1 to 2 minutes more.

5. Stir in the soy curls, paprika, fajita seasoning, and about 1 tablespoon of water. Cook the mixture for another 2 minutes, allowing the water to cook off, or until the veggies start to soften and the soy curls are heated through. Season to taste with salt and pepper.

6. Build your fajitas by topping each tortilla with the veggie filling, guacamole, jalapeño pepper, and any additional toppings, as desired.

Per serving: Calories: 291; Total fat: 13g; Total carbs: 37g; Fiber: 5g; Sugar: 5g; Protein: 10g; Sodium: 707mg

Chipotle Tofu and Veggie Burritos

SERVES 6

Prep time: 15 minutes
Cook time: 45 minutes

For the chipotle tofu

1 (14-ounce) block firm tofu, drained and pressed for at least 1 hour

2 or 3 chipotle peppers in adobo sauce, diced, plus 1 tablespoon of sauce

2 teaspoons freshly squeezed lime juice

½ teaspoon smoked paprika

¼ teaspoon salt

¼ teaspoon garlic powder

1 tablespoon vegetable oil, plus more as needed

Burritos are kind of perfect for meal prep. Sure, there are a lot of ingredients and your kitchen will get messy, but you can make a lot at the same time, filling your freezer with weeks' worth of future meals (see my tip). If you haven't cooked much with adobo or smoked paprika, you're in for a real treat. So much smoky flavor! To change up this recipe, sometimes I'll add sweet corn or throw in spiralized sweet potato with the peppers and onion. Looking for a shortcut? Many stores now carry seasoned, prebaked tofu in flavors like chipotle!

To make the chipotle tofu

1. Using your hands, crumble the tofu into a large bowl. Add the chipotle peppers, adobo sauce, lime juice, paprika, salt, and garlic powder. Mix well, being careful not to break down the tofu too much.

2. In a large skillet over medium-high heat, heat the vegetable oil until it shimmers.

3. Add the tofu and cook, stirring as needed, for 8 to 10 minutes. You want the tofu to be slightly browned. Add more oil, if needed. Remove the tofu from the skillet and set aside (no need to rinse the pan).

To make the burritos

1. Preheat the oven to 350°F. Coat a baking sheet with cooking spray.

CONTINUED

For the burritos

Nonstick cooking spray

2 bell peppers, any color

1 small sweet onion

2 to 3 tablespoons water

1 tablespoon fajita seasoning

2 teaspoons adobo sauce (from the can of peppers)

¼ teaspoon salt

⅛ teaspoon freshly ground black pepper

6 large tortillas

1 can pinto beans, rinsed and drained

1½ cups cooked rice

1 cup salsa

1 cup vegan cheddar shreds

2. Spiralize the bell peppers and onion using the Angel Hair blade and trim the spirals to 2-inch lengths.

3. Return the skillet to medium-high heat and heat the water. Add the bell pepper and onion spirals and fajita seasoning. Sauté for 5 to 6 minutes, or until the veggies are soft, adding more water as needed, but you want a dry pan when you're done.

4. Stir in the adobo sauce, salt, and pepper.

5. Build your burritos by topping each tortilla with the tofu, vegetables, pinto beans, rice, salsa, and cheddar shreds. Roll up the tortillas and place them on the prepared baking sheet, seam-side down. Cover the burritos with foil and bake for 25 minutes.

Preparation tip: Saving extra burritos for later use? Skip the baking, wrap them in foil, and freeze in a resealable freezer bag.

Per serving: Calories: 429; Total fat: 14g; Total carbs: 62g; Fiber: 10g; Sugar: 6g; Protein: 17g; Sodium: 1363mg

Desserts

Pumpkin-Spiced Apple Parfait, page 157

Chocolate-Beet Bundt Cake

SERVES 12
Prep time: 15 minutes
Cook time: 1 hour

Flour-infused nonstick
baking spray

2 medium beets

2 to 3 tablespoons water

1¾ cups all-purpose flour

1½ teaspoons baking
powder

½ teaspoon salt

2 vegan eggs (my
favorites are Follow Your
Heart and Just)

2 ounces dark chocolate,
melted

1½ cups granulated sugar

½ cup vegetable oil

½ cup unsweetened
applesauce

2 teaspoons vanilla extract

Powdered sugar,
for topping

I'm notoriously bad at baking, especially since moving to Colorado, where I've had to contend with high-altitude adjustments. I like to joke that *I have a bad altitude*, but for some reason, Bundt cakes have remained easy for me. I'm not sure if this is a fluke or something about the cake's cool shape, but I'm not going to question it. I'll just continue to enjoy simple, delicious cakes like this one. The subtle sweetness of the beet works amazingly well with chocolate—and they blend together so seamlessly, the beets are barely noticeable when you slice into it!

1. Preheat the oven to 350°F. Lightly coat a Bundt pan with flour-infused baking spray.

2. Spiralize the beets using the Angel Hair blade and trim the spirals to 3- to 4-inch lengths.

3. In a large nonstick skillet over medium-high heat, heat the water. Add the beet spirals and sauté for 8 to 10 minutes, until soft. Drain any remaining liquid, and set the spirals aside to cool.

4. In a small bowl, whisk together the flour, baking powder, and salt.

5. In a large bowl, whisk together the eggs, melted chocolate, sugar, vegetable oil, applesauce, and vanilla.

6. Slowly mix the dry ingredients into the wet ingredients, using a rubber spatula so you can scrape the sides clean. Don't overmix, just make sure everything is combined and there are no big lumps.

7. Fold in the beets and pour the mixture into the prepared pan.

8. Bake for 45 to 50 minutes, or until a toothpick inserted into the center comes out clean.

9. Let cool for 5 to 10 minutes before removing the cake from the pan. When cool, use a sifter to sprinkle the top of the cake with powdered sugar.

Per serving: Calories: 292; Total fat: 11g; Total carbs: 48g; Fiber: 2g; Sugar: 31g; Protein: 3g; Sodium: 131mg

NUT FREE, SOY FREE

Five-Spice Sweet Potato Bread

SERVES 10

Prep time: 15 minutes
Cook time: 1 hour

Flour-infused nonstick baking spray

1 medium sweet potato

2 to 3 tablespoons water

¼ cup unsweetened nondairy milk

1 teaspoon apple cider vinegar

1¾ cups all-purpose flour

1 cup granulated sugar

½ cup packed light brown sugar

1 tablespoon Chinese five-spice powder

2 teaspoons baking soda

½ teaspoon ground ginger

¼ teaspoon salt

2 vegan eggs (my favorites are Follow Your Heart and Just)

¼ cup unsweetened applesauce

1 teaspoon vanilla extract

One of my taste testers told me this bread tastes like Christmas—and I think she's right! Chinese five-spice powder is a blend of cinnamon, clove, fennel, star anise, and Szechuan peppercorns—so it's definitely spicy, but in a festive way. I like to serve this bread sliced, warm, with a little bit of vegan butter melted on top . . . but it would also be delicious with some Coconut Whipped Cream (page 176)!

1. Preheat the oven to 350°F. Lightly coat a 9½-by-5-inch loaf pan with flour-infused baking spray.

2. Spiralize the sweet potato with the Angel Hair blade and trim the spirals to 2- to 3-inch lengths.

3. In a large nonstick skillet over medium-high heat, heat the water. Add the sweet potato spirals to the pan and cook for 8 to 10 minutes, or until soft. Remove from the heat and set aside to cool.

4. In a small bowl, whisk together the milk and vinegar, and set aside.

5. In a medium bowl, whisk together the flour, sugars, five-spice powder, baking soda, ginger, and salt.

6. In a large bowl, whisk together the milk and vinegar mixture, eggs, applesauce, and vanilla. Slowly add the dry ingredients to the wet ingredients, stirring until completely combined. Don't overmix.

7. Fold in the sweet potato and pour the batter into the prepared pan.

8. Bake for 40 to 50 minutes, or until a toothpick inserted into the center comes out clean.

9. Let cool for 5 minutes in the pan, then transfer the loaf to a wire rack to cool completely.

Per serving: Calories: 201; Total fat: 1g; Total carbs: 45g; Fiber: 3g; Sugar: 22g; Protein: 4g; Sodium: 367mg

Triple Chocolate Zucchini Brownies

SERVES 16

Prep time: 20 minutes
Cook time: 35 minutes

For the brownies

Flour-infused nonstick baking spray

1 medium to large zucchini

1 vegan egg (my favorites are Follow Your Heart and Just)

1½ cups granulated sugar

½ cup vegetable oil

1½ teaspoons vanilla extract

2 cups all-purpose flour

½ cup unsweetened cocoa powder

1½ teaspoons baking powder

½ teaspoon ground cinnamon

¼ teaspoon salt

True story: I didn't like chocolate *at all* until I was in my thirties! My mom once, accidentally, bought me a chocolate birthday cake when I was seven or eight, and I was so indignant that I wouldn't even let *anyone else* eat it. That's how much I disliked chocolate. Thankfully, I saw the light, and these days I can't get enough of these super-chocolatey treats, which, of course, I justify by saying, *"But there are veggies in there!"*

To make the brownies

1. Preheat the oven to 350°F. Coat an 8-by-8-inch baking pan with flour-infused baking spray.

2. Spiralize the zucchini using the Angel Hair blade and trim the spirals to 4- to 5-inch lengths. Set aside.

3. In a large bowl, whisk together the egg, granulated sugar, vegetable oil, and vanilla.

4. In a medium bowl, stir together the flour, cocoa powder, baking powder, cinnamon, and salt. Slowly mix the dry ingredients into the wet ingredients, using a rubber spatula to scrape the sides of the bowl clean.

5. Stir in the zoodles and pour the batter into the prepared baking pan.

For the topping

3 tablespoons unsweetened cocoa powder

2 tablespoons vegan butter

1 cup powdered sugar

2 tablespoons unsweetened cashew milk

¼ teaspoon vanilla extract

¼ cup dark chocolate chips

6. Bake for 30 to 35 minutes, or until a toothpick inserted into the center comes out clean. Let cool before adding the topping.

To make the topping

1. In a small saucepan over medium-low heat, combine the cocoa powder and butter. Cook, stirring, just until melted. Remove from the heat immediately and let cool completely.

2. In a small bowl, stir together the powdered sugar, milk, and vanilla. Add the cooled chocolate mixture, and spread evenly over the top of the cooled brownies. Sprinkle with the chocolate chips.

Per serving: Calories: 226; Total fat: 10g; Total carbs: 35g; Fiber: 2g; Sugar: 20g; Protein: 3g; Sodium: 73mg

Beet Brownies

SERVES 16
Prep time: 15 minutes
Cook time: 50 minutes

Flour-infused nonstick
baking spray

2 medium to large beets

2 to 3 tablespoons water

1 cup dark chocolate
chunks

½ cup vegan butter

1¼ cups all-purpose flour

1½ teaspoons
baking powder

¼ teaspoon salt

1 vegan egg (my favorites
are Follow Your Heart
and Just)

1 cup sugar

2 teaspoons vanilla extract

Adding vegetables to foods in unexpected ways is, in my opinion, the best thing about spiralizing. These brownies are a little less rich than the Triple Chocolate Zucchini Brownies (page 146) but just as delicious!

1. Preheat the oven to 350°F. Coat an 8-by-8-inch baking pan with flour-infused baking spray.

2. Spiralize the beets using the Angel Hair blade and trim the spirals to 4- to 5-inch lengths.

3. In a large nonstick skillet over medium-high heat, heat the water. Add the beet spirals and sauté for 8 to 10 minutes, until soft.

4. In a double boiler, combine the chocolate chunks and butter and melt, stirring with a rubber spatula so you can scrape the sides clean, until completely combined. Remove from the heat and set aside.

5. In a medium bowl, stir together the flour, baking powder, and salt.

6. In a large bowl, whisk together the egg, sugar, and vanilla. Slowly add the dry ingredients to the wet ingredients, stirring until blended.

7. Fold in the beets and pour the batter into the prepared baking pan.

8. Bake for 30 to 40 minutes, or until a toothpick inserted into the center comes out clean. Let cool.

Per serving: Calories: 191; Total fat: 8g; Total carbs: 31g; Fiber: 2g; Sugar: 21g; Protein: 2g; Sodium: 118mg

Easy Pear Crisp

SERVES 4

Prep time: 10 minutes
Cook time: 40 minutes

For the filling

Flour-infused nonstick baking spray

4 large pears

⅔ cup packed light brown sugar

2 teaspoons freshly squeezed lemon juice

¼ teaspoon salt

For the topping

1½ cups all-purpose flour

½ cup packed light brown sugar

½ teaspoon ground cinnamon

¼ teaspoon ground allspice

¼ teaspoon ground nutmeg

½ cup chopped walnuts

½ cup vegan butter, melted

Coconut Whipped Cream (page 176), for topping

Vegan vanilla ice cream, for topping

I am very well known (at least to myself) for my apple crisp recipe. It's made in a pressure cooker with bourbon, though, so it's not for everyone. When I decided to create a baked version, I knew I wanted to use a different fruit, and pear was the perfect choice!

To make the filling

1. Preheat the oven to 350°F. Lightly spritz a pie pan with flour-infused baking spray. Set aside.

2. Spiralize the pears using the Curly Fry blade, and toss in a large bowl with the brown sugar, lemon juice, and salt.

3. Transfer the pear mixture to the prepared pie pan, using the back of a spoon to smooth the mixture and pack it down.

To make the topping

In a large bowl, stir together the flour, brown sugar, cinnamon, allspice, nutmeg, and walnuts. Pour the melted butter over the top, while stirring, until the topping is mixed together. Add the topping to the pears; use the back of a spoon to smooth it evenly over the pear mixture.

To finish the crisp

Bake for 35 to 40 minutes, or until the topping is crisp and golden. Serve warm or at room temperature, topped with the whipped cream and ice cream.

Per serving: Calories: 841; Total fat: 33g; Total carbs: 134g; Fiber: 9g; Sugar: 81g; Protein: 8g; Sodium: 417mg

Spiced Pear and Apple Pie

SERVES 8

Prep time: 20 minutes
Cook time: 45 minutes

4 medium to large apples

3 medium pears

1 tablespoon freshly
squeezed lemon juice

2 store-bought or
homemade vegan pie
dough rounds

3 tablespoons cornstarch

1 teaspoon ground
cinnamon

1 teaspoon vanilla extract

¾ teaspoon ground
ginger

½ teaspoon ground
allspice

½ teaspoon ground
nutmeg

¼ teaspoon salt

2 tablespoons vegan
butter, cold, each
tablespoon cut into
quarters

Coconut Whipped Cream
(page 176), for topping
(optional)

Vegan vanilla ice cream,
for topping (optional)

This spiced version of a traditional apple pie ties in all
my favorite autumnal flavors, including pear! Be sure to
choose pears just a little bit shy of fully ripe (firm, but
not hard), as they'll work better for spiralizing.

1. Preheat the oven to 375°F.

2. Spiralize the apples and pears using the Curly Fry
   blade and trim to 4- to 5-inch lengths. Transfer the
   spirals to a large bowl and toss with the lemon juice.
   Set aside.

3. Place one round of dough in a 9-inch pie pan and
   trim the edges. Set aside.

4. Add the cornstarch, cinnamon, vanilla, ginger,
   allspice, nutmeg, and salt to the fruit spirals, and mix
   well to combine. Pour the filling into the pie pan.
   Top with the butter, and place the second round of
   dough on top, crimping the edges to seal. Cut slits
   in the top of the crust and cover the edges with
   foil. Bake for 35 to 45 minutes, or until the crust is
   golden and the fruit filling is bubbly. Remove the foil
   for the last 10 minutes of baking time. Serve topped
   with the Coconut Whipped Cream and vegan vanilla
   ice cream, if desired.

Per serving: Calories: 297; Total fat: 14g; Total carbs:
44g; Fiber: 5g; Sugar: 19g; Protein: 2g; Sodium: 314mg

Fried Apple Fritters

SERVES 4

Prep time: 15 minutes
Cook time: 10 minutes

1 cup all-purpose flour

¼ cup granulated sugar

1½ teaspoons
baking powder

½ teaspoon ground
cinnamon

¼ teaspoon salt

1 vegan egg (my favorites
are Follow Your Heart
and Just)

⅓ cup nondairy milk

½ teaspoon vanilla extract

2 small apples (I use
1 Granny Smith and
1 Pink Lady)

1 cup canola oil

Powdered sugar,
for dusting

Sure, you can buy apple fritters at the store. But they'll never be as sweet, crispy, or satisfying as fritters you make yourself. Plus, your kitchen will smell like autumn when you fry these up! I recommend using two kinds of apples and mixing them together.

1. In a small bowl, stir together the flour, granulated sugar, baking powder, cinnamon, and salt.

2. In a large bowl, whisk together the egg, milk, and vanilla. Slowly stir the dry ingredients into the wet ingredients. Set aside.

3. Spiralize the apples using the Curly Fry blade and trim the spirals to 1- to 2-inch lengths. Gently fold the spirals into the batter.

4. In a large heavy-bottomed skillet over medium-high heat, heat the oil until it shimmers. Line a plate with paper towels and set aside.

5. Drop a small bit of the batter into the oil to test it. You want it to sizzle, rise to the top of the oil, and slowly brown. If it starts to burn, turn down the heat, wait a few minutes, and try again.

6. When the oil is ready, drop in about 1 teaspoon of batter at a time. Cook each fritter for about 2 minutes, flipping halfway through. Transfer the fried fritters to the prepared plate to drain off the excess oil.

7. Sprinkle with powdered sugar before serving.

Per serving: Calories: 384; Total fat: 15g; Total carbs: 61g; Fiber: 5g; Sugar: 28g; Protein: 4g; Sodium: 192mg

Chili-Mango Cheesecake Bites

SERVES 9
Prep time: 15 minutes
Cook time: 20 minutes

1 (8-ounce) tube Pillsbury crescent rolls

1 large, firm, peeled mango

⅛ teaspoon chili powder

4 ounces vegan cream cheese, at room temperature

2 tablespoons granulated sugar

1 tablespoon vegan butter, melted

1 tablespoon turbinado sugar

Spiralizing a mango isn't as straightforward as other fruits because of its large pit, but it can be done! Choose large mangos that are just shy of completely ripe: You want them to be firm but not hard. I think you'll really enjoy their flavor in this dessert—the sweet creaminess of the "cheesecake" with the spicy sweetness of the chili and mango is an amazing combination.

1. Preheat the oven to 350°F.

2. Spread out the crescent roll dough in one sheet (do not break apart) onto an ungreased baking pan. Pinch the seams together to make it a uniform dough.

3. Cut away large chunks of the mango from the pit. Spiralize the chunks using the Angel Hair blade; you'll get 1- to 2-inch strands, which are perfect. When you have a heaping ½ cup, transfer the mango strands to a small bowl and stir in the chili powder. Set aside.

4. In another small bowl, stir together the cream cheese and granulated sugar. Spread the mixture over half of the crescent roll sheet, being careful to spread it evenly (don't put more in the center). Top the mixture with the chili and mango. Fold the other side of the crescent sheet over to cover the filling, and pinch together the outer edges.

5. Brush the melted butter over the top, and sprinkle with the turbinado sugar. Bake for 15 to 20 minutes, or until golden brown. Let sit for a few minutes before slicing and serving.

Per serving: Calories: 183; Total fat: 10g; Total carbs: 21g; Fiber: 2g; Sugar: 11g; Protein: 3g; Sodium: 262mg

Lemon-Mango Tartlets

MAKES 15 TARTLETS
Prep time: 10 minutes
Cook time: 5 minutes

Juice of 2 medium lemons
(about ⅓ cup)

½ cup sugar

½ cup water

2 tablespoons cornstarch

⅛ teaspoon ground
turmeric

2 large, firm but not hard,
peeled mangos

45 mini frozen phyllo
cups, thawed

Zest of 2 medium lemons

These tiny tartlets are terrifically tart! But not too tart . . .
the sweetness of the mango provides a wonderful
balance. I like to make these for parties where there's a
lot of mingling, because they're so easy to pop in your
mouth and as you keep moving. The filling can be made
ahead of time, but don't layer it into the phyllo shells until
it's time to serve. And, keep in mind, if you're using premade shells that aren't "mini," the filling won't go as far.

1. In a medium saucepan over medium heat, combine
    the lemon juice, sugar, water, cornstarch, and tur-
    meric. Whisk together until completely smooth, and
    let the mixture come to a simmer. Cook, stirring con-
    stantly with a rubber spatula and watching closely, as
    the mixture can suddenly go from a liquid to a thick
    gel. The combined heating and simmering time will be
    about 5 minutes. Remove from the heat and let cool.

2. Cut away large chunks of mango from the pit and
    spiralize them using the Angel Hair blade. The
    chunks will break apart, so there's no need to cut
    them into small pieces. You want about ⅔ cup.

3. When the lemon mixture is cool, fill each phyllo cup
    with about 1 teaspoon of the mixture.

4. Top with the mango and a small amount of lemon
    zest. Serve chilled or at room temperature.

Ingredient tip: I use the Athens brand of mini phyllo
cups. They're available in most grocery stores in the
frozen dessert section.

Per serving (1 tartlet): Calories: 115; Total fat: 3g; Total
carbs: 22g; Fiber: 1g; Sugar: 13g; Protein: 1g; Sodium: 36mg

Coconut–Plantain Rice Pudding

SERVES 4

Prep time: 10 minutes
Cook time: 40 minutes

2 cups cooked jasmine rice, cold

1 to 1½ cups nondairy milk, divided

1 can full-fat coconut milk

⅓ cup pure maple syrup

¼ teaspoon salt

1 ripe yet firm plantain

½ teaspoon vanilla extract

½ cup coconut flakes, sweetened or unsweetened

Did you know you can make rice pudding with any variety of rice? It's true. You can even make it with brown rice—it just won't be as sweet. I like to use jasmine or basmati rice; I find they work best and always satisfy my sweet tooth. If you want to lighten up this recipe, use lite coconut milk; it just won't be quite as rich and creamy.

1. In a medium saucepan over medium heat, stir together the cold rice, 1 cup of milk, the coconut milk, maple syrup, and salt. Simmer for 25 to 30 minutes, until thickened, stirring frequently to avoid sticking and burning.

2. Spiralize the plantain using the Angel Hair blade and trim the spirals to 1-inch lengths. Stir the plantain spirals and vanilla into the rice pudding, and cook for 5 to 6 minutes more, adding the remaining ½ cup milk, if needed, for consistency.

3. Spoon the pudding into bowls, and top with the coconut flakes.

Per serving: Calories: 459; Total fat: 30g; Total carbs: 50g; Fiber: 5g; Sugar: 27g; Protein: 4g; Sodium: 229mg

Cherry-Pear Parfait

SERVES 4

Prep time: 15 minutes

1½ cups vegan vanilla yogurt

3 tablespoons powdered sugar

½ cup cherries, pitted and sliced, plus 4 whole pitted cherries

2 pears

6 vegan graham crackers, crumbled (1 to 1½ cups)

Coconut Whipped Cream (page 176), for topping

Anything served in a parfait glass is instantly fancy, right? That's part of what makes these desserts such a fun way to end a special meal or to make an ordinary meal special! Make someone's day by serving them a parfait that literally has a cherry on top. Just be sure to check your ingredients, as many brands of graham crackers contain honey.

1. In a medium bowl, stir together the yogurt, sugar, and cherries.

2. Spiralize the pears using the Angel Hair blade and trim the spirals to 2- to 3-inch lengths.

3. In each of four parfait glasses, evenly layer one-eighth of the pears, one-eighth of the graham crackers, and about 3 tablespoons of yogurt. Repeat the layers—pears, graham crackers, and yogurt—until you've used all the ingredients.

4. Top with a scoop of whipped cream and a cherry!

Serving tip: You can refrigerate these for 5 to 10 minutes, if needed, but any longer and you risk the graham crackers getting soggy.

Per serving: Calories: 187; Total fat: 6g; Total carbs: 57g; Fiber: 4g; Sugar: 35g; Protein: 5g; Sodium: 231mg

Pumpkin-Spiced Apple Parfait

SERVES 4

Prep time: 10 minutes

Cook time: 10 minutes

For the apple filling

2 medium apples

2 teaspoons freshly squeezed lemon juice

1 tablespoon pure maple syrup

3 teaspoons all-purpose flour

1½ teaspoons pumpkin pie spice

For the parfaits

2 cups vegan vanilla yogurt

1½ cups granola

Coconut Whipped Cream (page 176), for topping

Okay, okay, the Coconut Whipped Cream isn't necessarily *required* to make this dessert drool-worthy, but I feel like you might as well go all out. Plus, the apple filling is basically a combination of apple pie and pumpkin pie, both of which pair so well with sweet whipped topping. Have I talked you into it yet? I do recommend using unsweetened granola, as there's already a lot of sweetness in this dish.

To make the apple filling

1. Spiralize the apples using the Fine Shred blade and trim the spirals to 2- to 3-inch lengths. Transfer the spirals to a medium saucepan, and stir in the lemon juice until coated.

2. Place the saucepan over medium-low heat, and stir in the maple syrup, flour, and pumpkin pie spice. Cook for 8 to 10 minutes, or until the apples are soft. Set aside.

CONTINUED

To make the parfaits

1. In each of four parfait glasses or bowls, layer ¼ cup of yogurt, one-eighth of the apple mixture, and about 3 tablespoons of granola. Repeat the layers— yogurt, apple mixture, and granola—until you've used all the ingredients.

2. Top with a scoop of whipped cream. Serve immediately.

Per serving: Calories: 457; Total fat: 25g; Total carbs: 56g; Fiber: 4g; Sugar: 33g; Protein: 5g; Sodium: 12mg

"Apple Pie" Sundaes

SERVES 4
Prep time: 10 minutes
Cook time: 7 minutes

⅓ cup water

1 teaspoon cornstarch

4 large apples

¼ cup vegan butter

2 tablespoons pure maple syrup

½ teaspoon ground nutmeg

½ teaspoon ground cinnamon

3 cups vegan vanilla ice cream

1 cup granola

Coconut Whipped Cream (page 176), for topping

I don't have a huge sweet tooth, but when I do indulge, it's usually ice cream or fruit pie. This ice cream sundae brings both of those delicious treats together in the best possible way. Do be mindful with your apple choices! I recommend mixing two types, something sweet like Honeycrisp or Pink Lady with something tart like a Granny Smith.

1. In a small bowl, whisk together the water and cornstarch until the cornstarch dissolves. Set the slurry aside while you prepare the apples.

2. Spiralize the apples using the Fine Shred blade.

3. In a large saucepan over medium heat, melt the butter.

4. Add the apple spirals and cook for 2 to 3 minutes, until they begin to soften.

5. Add the cornstarch slurry, maple syrup, nutmeg, and cinnamon. Cook, stirring frequently, for 3 to 4 minutes. When the sauce is thick and the apples are soft, like they would be in a pie, they're done. Remove from the heat and let cool for 1 to 2 minutes.

6. Divide the ice cream evenly among four bowls and top each with the apple mixture. Sprinkle with granola, and top with the whipped cream. Serve immediately.

Per serving: Calories: 461; Total fat: 19g; Total carbs: 74g; Fiber: 8g; Sugar: 54g; Protein: 4g; Sodium: 214mg

Spicy-Sweet Strawberry Mango Sorbet Sundaes

SERVES 4

Prep time: 10 minutes

3 tablespoons Tapatío hot sauce, or similar

3 tablespoons agave

2 large, peeled mangos

4 cups vegan strawberry sorbet

1 cup sliced strawberries

Spicy and sweet is a combination you see a lot in savory dishes, even in my Sweet 'n' Spicy Fruit Salad (page 100), but I really think spicy is too often overlooked when it comes to desserts. If you think this may be a bit out of your comfort zone, reduce the amount of hot sauce to just 1 or 2 teaspoons and work your way up.

1. In a small bowl, stir together the hot sauce and agave.

2. Cut away chunks of the mango from the pit and spiralize using the Angel Hair blade.

3. Divide the strawberry sorbet evenly among four bowls, and top with the mango and sliced strawberries.

4. Drizzle with the spicy-sweet sauce.

Per serving: Calories: 278; Total fat: 1g; Total carbs: 71g; Fiber: 5g; Sugar: 58g; Protein: 2g; Sodium: 95mg

Coconut-Pear Sundaes with Fudge Sauce

SERVES 4

Prep time: 15 minutes

Cook time: 5 minutes

These sundaes remind me of a certain candy bar I used to love as a child, but with pear! I usually make this with a coconut milk–based ice cream, but any vegan ice cream will work.

For the fudge sauce

2½ tablespoons vegan butter

2 tablespoons cocoa powder

2 tablespoons light brown sugar

¼ cup unsweetened cashew milk

¼ cup brown rice syrup

½ cup dark chocolate chunks

1 teaspoon vanilla extract

Pinch salt

For the sundaes

1 large pear

3 cups vegan vanilla ice cream, slightly softened

½ cup sweetened coconut flakes

½ cup chopped toasted almonds

To make the fudge sauce

1. In a medium saucepan, combine the butter, cocoa powder, brown sugar, milk, and rice syrup. Place the pan over medium-high heat and bring the mixture to a boil. Reduce the heat to low and simmer for 4 to 5 minutes, whisking constantly. It's done when it starts to thicken. Remove the pan from the heat.

2. Stir in the chocolate chunks, vanilla, and salt. Switch to a rubber spatula and keep stirring, scraping down the sides of the pan. When the sauce is smooth, set aside and let cool and thicken for at least 10 minutes.

To make the sundaes

1. Spiralize the pear using the Angel Hair blade and trim the spirals to 1- to 2-inch lengths.

2. Transfer the slightly softened ice cream to a large bowl and add the coconut and almonds. Use a sturdy spoon to stir them into the ice cream. Divide the ice cream evenly among four bowls.

3. Top the ice cream with pear spirals and fudge sauce.

Per serving: Calories: 509; Total fat: 27g; Total carbs: 70g; Fiber: 6g; Sugar: 53g; Protein: 7g; Sodium: 264mg

Drinks

Mango-Habanero Seltzer Water, page 166

Fruity Iced Tea

SERVES 2

Prep time: 10 minutes, plus 12 hours to chill

2 large sweet apples, such as Honeycrisp

½ small cucumber

4 tea bags, any brand

4 cups water

1 to 2 tablespoons simple syrup (optional)

Hosting a picnic or barbecue? Here's an easy way to show your guests what a talented host you are! Anyone can serve plain iced tea, but yours is fancy and flavorful. Feeling extra? Spiralize additional apples to put in the cups!

1. Spiralize the apples and cucumber using the Angel Hair blade. Put the spirals in a large pitcher, and add the tea bags and water. Refrigerate for at least 12 hours.

2. Remove and discard the tea bags. Stir in the simple syrup (if using), or enjoy with just the natural fruit sweetness, like I do!

Per serving: Calories: 127; Total fat: 1g; Total carbs: 34g; Fiber: 6g; Sugar: 25g; Protein: 1g; Sodium: 4mg

Cucumber-and-Blueberry-Infused Water

SERVES 4

Prep time: 5 minutes, plus 12 hours to chill

1 small cucumber

½ cup fresh blueberries

3 thin slices lemon

Blueberry, lemon, and cucumber are a popular combination in detox water, but to me, they just taste good! Infused water is a great way to ensure you're staying hydrated if you're someone who gets bored with plain old tap water. I recommend keeping a pitcher in your refrigerator at all times!

1. Spiralize the cucumber using the Coarse Wavy blade and put the spirals in a large pitcher.

2. Add the blueberries and lemon slices and fill the pitcher with water. Cover and refrigerate for 12 hours.

3. Remove the fruit and enjoy.

Per serving: Calories: 22; Total fat: 0g; Total carbs: 5g; Fiber: 1g; Sugar: 3g; Protein: 1g; Sodium: 2mg

Mango-Habanero Seltzer Water

SERVES 2

Prep time: 10 minutes

2 mangos, peeled, 1 whole to spiralize and 1 chopped into small pieces (about 1 cup)

1 Honeycrisp apple

½ small habanero pepper, stemmed, seeded, and cut into 2 or 3 pieces

1 quart seltzer water

1 teaspoon agave (optional)

Flavored seltzer water is all the rage right now. From lemon, lime, and *pamplemousse* (what *is* that, even?) to cherry and peach . . . you have lots of choices. But sometimes, when you're sitting outside on a beautiful summer day with a book, you want something a little spicy. This is such a fun flavor, anyone you serve it to will be impressed by your originality!

1. Cut away chunks of the whole mango from the pit and spiralize them using the Angel Hair blade. Set aside.

2. Spiralize the apple using the Angel Hair blade and trim the spirals to 3- to 4-inch lengths.

3. In a large martini shaker, combine the chopped mango and habanero. Muddle until soft.

4. Add the seltzer water and agave (if using). Cover and mix gently.

5. Fill two pint glasses halfway with ice, and add the spiralized apple and spiralized mango.

6. With the strainer on the shaker, pour the water into the glasses and enjoy!

Serving tip: A shot of tequila or mango-flavored rum would turn this seltzer into a delicious cocktail!

Per serving: Calories: 261; Total fat: 2g; Total carbs: 66g; Fiber: 8g; Sugar: 57g; Protein: 3g; Sodium: 4mg

Cucumber Mojitos

SERVES 2

Prep time: 10 minutes

½ small cucumber

3 ounces light rum

10 fresh mint leaves, divided

2 teaspoons freshly squeezed lime juice

2 teaspoons simple syrup

8 ounces club soda

There was a time when I thought mojitos were too complicated to make myself. I loved their fresh, minty flavor, so I'd order them in bars and on vacation—but I never got to enjoy them at home. Turns out they're really not that complicated! This recipe makes two servings, but you can easily double it (if your cocktail shaker is large enough) and serve a small crowd. I highly recommend enjoying these outside in the sun, with good friends or a good book.

1. Spiralize the cucumber using the Angel Hair blade and trim the spirals to 4-inch lengths. Set aside.

2. In a cocktail shaker, muddle the rum and 6 mint leaves. Add the lime juice and simple syrup. Cover the shaker and give it a shake or two.

3. Fill two glasses with ice and the spiralized cucumber. With the strainer on, divide the rum mix between the two glasses.

4. Top off the glasses with club soda and the remaining mint leaves.

Preparation tip: I love the flavor of cucumber, but I know it can be strong. I use a full one-fourth of a small cucumber in each drink; if you're not sure, start off with just one-eighth.

Per serving: Calories: 139; Total fat: 0g; Total carbs: 10g; Fiber: 1g; Sugar: 2g; Protein: 1g; Sodium: 34mg

Vodka Spritzer with Apple and Jicama

SERVES 4

Prep time: 10 minutes

½ cup vodka

2 tablespoons simple syrup

1 teaspoon freshly squeezed lime juice

1 small jicama (about the size of an apple), rind removed

1 medium apple

2 cups club soda

Vodka spritzers are one of my favorite cocktails because they're simple to make, yet they can be as fancy and decadent as you like! This version has a mild sweetness from the apple and jicama—although the exact flavor will depend on what variety of apple you use. I prefer something sweet like a Honeycrisp, but if you want to add more of a tart flavor, go with Granny Smith.

1. In a cocktail shaker, combine the vodka, simple syrup, and lime juice.

2. Spiralize the jicama and apple using the Angel Hair blade; no need to trim the spirals.

3. Fill four glasses with ice and the jicama and apple spirals. Add the vodka mixture to each glass and top off with club soda.

Serving tip: Skipping the alcohol? Increase the amount of club soda, but leave everything else the same.

Per serving: Calories: 161; Total fat: 0g; Total carbs: 26g; Fiber: 6g; Sugar: 8g; Protein: 1g; Sodium: 37mg

Staples + Sauces

Coconut Whipped Cream, page 176

Alfredo Sauce

MAKES ABOUT 2 CUPS
Prep time: 10 minutes
Cook time: 6 to 7 minutes
(optional)

1 (14-ounce) package
soft tofu, drained but not
pressed

⅓ cup nutritional yeast

¼ cup unsweetened soy
or cashew milk

½ teaspoon salt

¼ teaspoon garlic powder

¼ teaspoon Italian
seasoning

½ cup vegan mozzarella
shreds (optional)

This is my go-to Alfredo sauce that I use on everything from zoodles to pasta to Super Squash Lasagna with White Sauce (page 123), which includes both! You may notice you need a little less sauce with veggie noodles than you're used to with pasta, because they just don't soak it up as much. Personally, I like my dishes saucy (probably because I'm also serving garlic bread or dinner rolls), so I still use the same amount, but use your judgment.

1. In a food processor or blender, combine the tofu, nutritional yeast, milk, salt, garlic powder, and Italian seasoning. Blend until smooth.

2. If using the mozzarella, transfer the sauce to a small saucepan over medium-low heat. Cook for 4 to 5 minutes, then add the cheese. Cook, stirring, until melted, 1 to 2 minutes more. This sauce will keep, refrigerated in an airtight container, for 3 to 4 days.

Preparation tip: Using this sauce in a baked recipe? No need to heat it. Skip step 2 and add it directly to your dish.

Per serving (½ cup): Calories: 81; Total fat: 4g; Total carbs: 4g; Fiber: 1g; Sugar: 1g; Protein: 9g; Sodium: 254mg

Tofu Ricotta

MAKES ABOUT 2 CUPS
Prep time: 10 minutes

1 (14-ounce) block firm tofu, drained and pressed for 5 to 10 minutes

⅓ cup nutritional yeast

1 tablespoon olive oil

2 teaspoons garlic powder

2 teaspoons onion powder

2 teaspoons dried oregano

2 tablespoons unsweetened nondairy milk

1 teaspoon dried basil

1 teaspoon salt

⅛ teaspoon freshly ground black pepper

I make this ricotta all the time, because it has so many uses! In this book alone, you can use it with Roasted Beet Pizza (page 110), Sausage and Zucchini Noodle Lasagna Casserole (page 121), and even Tex-Mex Potato Noodle Pie (page 119). I love how quick and easy it is to whip up! Although this recipe does make enough for your standard lasagna or stuffed shell recipe, here's a secret: When I want my dish to be extra decadent, I double the ricotta. Try it in your next pan of lasagna—you won't be sorry!

In a food processor, combine the tofu, nutritional yeast, oil, garlic powder, onion powder, oregano, milk, basil, salt, and pepper. Pulse until mixed. Don't overmix—you don't want the tofu to turn to mush. This will keep, refrigerated in an airtight container, for 3 to 4 days.

Per serving (¼ cup): Calories: 64; Total fat: 4g; Total carbs: 3g; Fiber: 1g; Sugar: 1g; Protein: 5g; Sodium: 247mg

Garlicky Lemon Cream Sauce

MAKES 1½ CUPS
Prep time: 5 minutes
Cook time: 10 minutes

3 tablespoons vegan
butter

4 garlic cloves, minced

3 tablespoons
all-purpose flour

1½ cups unsweetened
nondairy milk

½ teaspoon salt

Juice of 1 lemon

Zest of 1 lemon

This is one of my very favorite sauces. Ever. It's simple and easy to make, with ingredients you probably have on hand, yet it's so versatile! Use it as-is in the Quinoa Veggie Bowl with Garlicky Lemon Cream Sauce (page 38), or spice it up with some hot sauce when you whip up the Garlicky Chili Cauliflower Rice Bowl (page 41). Garlic and lemon go well together, and with so many vegetables, this sauce's potential is limited only by your imagination!

1. In a small saucepan over medium heat, melt the butter.

2. Add the garlic and sauté for 3 minutes.

3. Whisk in the flour and cook for 2 to 3 minutes. (This is your roux.)

4. Stir in the milk, salt, and lemon juice, whisking until blended. Bring the sauce to a boil, reduce the heat to low, and simmer for 2 to 3 minutes, or until it's thickened, stirring frequently.

5. Use the lemon zest to garnish when plating.

6. This sauce will keep, refrigerated in an airtight container, for 3 to 4 days.

Per serving (¼ cup): Calories: 77; Total fat: 6g; Total carbs: 5g; Fiber: 1g; Sugar: 0g; Protein: 1g; Sodium: 341mg

Ranch Dressing

SERVES 8

Prep time: 10 minutes,
plus overnight soaking

½ cup unsweetened
nondairy milk

2½ teaspoons apple cider
vinegar, divided

¾ cup raw cashews,
soaked overnight in water,
drained, and rinsed

1 teaspoon garlic powder

½ teaspoon onion powder

½ teaspoon agave

¼ teaspoon salt

⅛ teaspoon freshly
ground black pepper

2 teaspoons chopped
fresh parsley

1 teaspoon chopped
fresh dill

There weren't any vegan ranch dressings when I first gave up dairy, which was a big disappointment. Now there are lots of brands to choose from, but I still think whipping up a batch of your own is the best way to make sure you don't run out—which is a serious risk when you consider how many uses there are for this dressing, like with Spicy Southwestern Parsnip Fries (page 58) and Buffalo Tofu Pizza with Cauliflower Crust (page 106)!

1. In a small bowl, whisk together the milk and 1½ teaspoons of vinegar. Let the mixture sit for a few minutes, then pour into a blender.

2. Add the remaining 1 teaspoon of vinegar, the cashews, garlic powder, onion powder, agave, salt, and pepper. Blend until completely smooth.

3. Add the parsley and dill. Pulse 2 to 3 times to combine. Refrigerate in an airtight container until ready to use; it will keep refrigerated in an airtight container for 3 to 4 days.

Per serving: Calories: 78; Total fat: 5g; Total carbs: 5g; Fiber: 1g; Sugar: 1g; Protein: 2g; Sodium: 83mg

Coconut Whipped Cream

SERVES 4 TO 6
Prep time: 5 minutes,
plus overnight chilling

1 (14-ounce) can full-fat
coconut milk, refrigerated
overnight

¼ cup powdered sugar

½ teaspoon vanilla extract

Here is a super-simple dessert topping that you can literally whip up in minutes! I keep a can of full-fat coconut milk in the refrigerator at all times just for dessert emergencies (a real thing!). I recommend using a brand-name (not store-brand) coconut milk for this, as brand-name milks tend to have better results.

1. Without shaking it, open the can of coconut milk and scoop the solidified cream into a chilled metal mixing bowl. Using a handheld electric mixer, whip for 30 to 45 seconds, or until it becomes creamy and smooth.

2. Add the sugar and vanilla. Continue to whip for 30 to 60 seconds more, until completely smooth. Refrigerate the whipped cream until you're ready to use it; it'll firm more as it chills. Unused coconut whipped cream will keep, refrigerated in an airtight container, for a week . . . unless you eat it first!

Per serving: Calories: 239; Total fat: 20g; Total carbs: 14g; Fiber: 0g; Sugar: 7g; Protein: 2g; Sodium: 0mg

Measurement Conversions

OVEN TEMPERATURES

Fahrenheit	Celsius (approximate)
250°F	120°C
300°F	150°C
325°F	165°C
350°F	180°C
375°F	190°C
400°F	200°C
425°F	220°C
450°F	230°C

VOLUME EQUIVALENTS (LIQUID)

US Standard	US Standard (ounces)	Metric (approximate)
2 tablespoons	1 fl. oz.	30 mL
¼ cup	2 fl. oz.	60 mL
½ cup	4 fl. oz.	120 mL
1 cup	8 fl. oz.	240 mL
1½ cups	12 fl. oz.	355 mL
2 cups or 1 pint	16 fl. oz.	475 mL
4 cups or 1 quart	32 fl. oz.	1 L
1 gallon	128 fl. oz.	4 L

WEIGHT EQUIVALENTS

US Standard	Metric (approximate)
½ ounce	15 g
1 ounce	30 g
2 ounces	60 g
4 ounces	115 g
8 ounces	225 g
12 ounces	340 g
16 ounces or 1 pound	455 g

VOLUME EQUIVALENTS (DRY)

US Standard	Metric (approximate)
⅛ teaspoon	0.5 mL
¼ teaspoon	1 mL
½ teaspoon	2 mL
¾ teaspoon	4 mL
1 teaspoon	5 mL
1 tablespoon	15 mL
¼ cup	59 mL
⅓ cup	79 mL
½ cup	118 mL
⅔ cup	156 mL
¾ cup	177 mL
1 cup	235 mL
2 cups or 1 pint	475 mL
3 cups	700 mL
4 cups or 1 quart	1 L

Resources

How home cooks found answers to their questions before the Internet, I do not know. Thankfully, we don't have that problem! Here are some websites that are chock-full of information, ideas, and tips on vegan cooking in general, and spiralizing in particular:

- Cadry's Kitchen, a blog full of great recipes and tips: CadrysKitchen.com

- Helpful tips on spiralizing for beginners: Downshiftology.com /spiralizer-beginners-guide

- JL Goes Vegan, an amazing resource for vegans and the vegan-curious: JLGoesVegan.com

- Vegan Crunk offers a fun, fresh look at vegan foods, products, and techniques: VeganCrunk.blogspot.com

- Vegan recipes and resources from a world-famous chef: JazzyVegetarian.com /blog

- More great tips on spiralizing: Plated.com/morsel/guide-to-spiralizing

- Ask questions and find answers on everything vegan: Reddit.com/r/vegan

And when you're looking for the latest and greatest vegan products online, these websites are my go-tos:

- VeganCuts.com/shop

- Vegan.com/grocery

- VeganEssentials.com

Index

Acknowledgments

First and foremost, thank you to my mom. She's the reason I'm as strong as I am and why I refuse to back down from any challenge. I learned from the best! To Elmer and Frankie, my faithful companions, who spent every moment of this project in the kitchen with me. To Denise Lindom, who not only helped me brainstorm, chop, stir, and bake but also patched up my wounds. And to Tony—I hope they have really good sugar cookies wherever you are.

A huge shout-out to my recipe testers, all of whom have spiraled their way into my heart forever: Jacquie Astemborski, Susan Burgmaier, Donna Gibson, Sonali Hemachandra, Jamie Hostetter, Kirsten Jasek-Rysdahl, Jessica Loalbo, Kathy Monteiro, and Cynthia Thayer—this book wouldn't be the same without your insights and suggestions, and I am so thankful to you!

Finally, a thousand thank-yous to my editor Samantha Barbaro and everyone at Callisto Media who made this book happen!

About the Author

BARB MUSICK lives in Colorado with her pack of rescue pets. She shares her adventures and love of food, travel, and animals on her blog, *That Was Vegan?*, along with vegan recipes everyone will love. Visit her *at ThatWasVegan.com.*

CPSIA information can be obtained
at www.ICGtesting.com
Printed in the USA
BVHW021110180919
558760BV00017B/493/P